MEVAGISSEY

David Weston

Epic, Over & Out
Newquay Padstow Bude Launceston

David Weston Gallery

Mevagissey Cornwall England

ISBN 0 9517290 4 7

Printed by Blackfords of Cornwall
Holmbush, St. Austell PL25 3JL

Contents

Illustrations

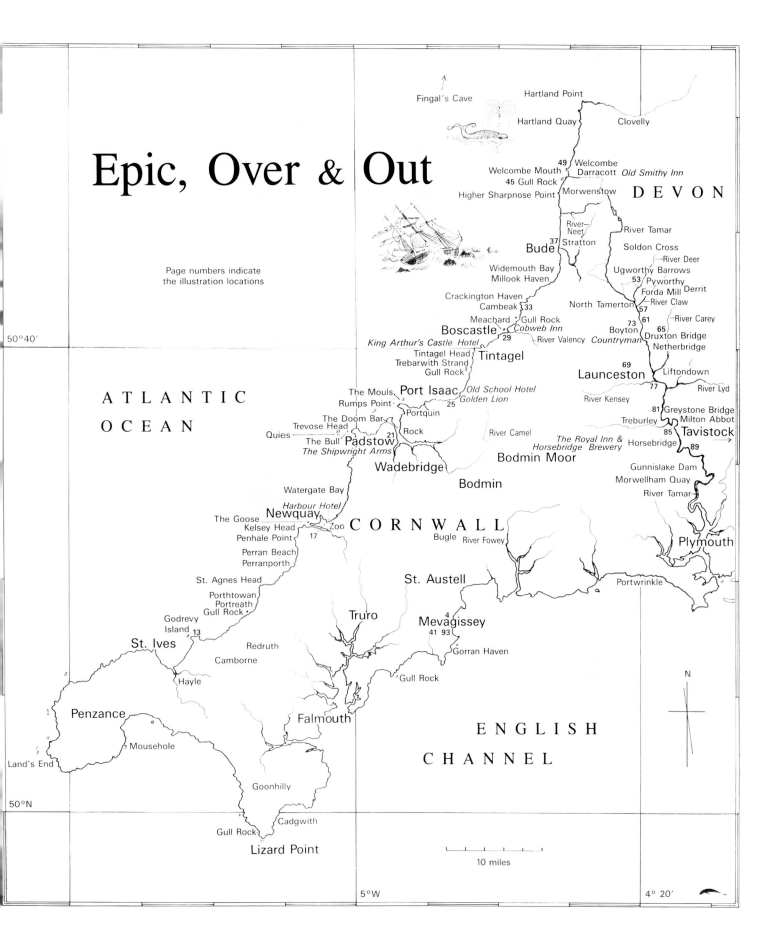

Epic, Over & Out

Page numbers indicate
the illustration locations

Fingal's Cave

Hartland Point

Hartland Quay   Clovelly

49 Welcombe
Welcombe Mouth   Darracott   *Old Smithy Inn*
45 Gull Rock
Higher Sharpnose Point   Morwenstow   D E V O N

River
Neet   River Tamar
37   Stratton   Soldon Cross
Bude   River Deer
Widemouth Bay   Ugworthy Barrows
Millook Haven   53 Pyworthy
Forda Mill Derrit
Crackington Haven   North Tamerton   River Claw
Cambeak 33   57
Meachard ; Gull Rock   73   River Carey
Boscastle   *Cobweb Inn*   Boyton   61
King Arthur's Castle Hotel   29   River Valency *Countryman*   65
Druxton Bridge
Tintagel Head   Netherbridge
Trebarwith Strand   Tintagel
Gull Rock   69
Launceston   Liftondown

The Mouls   Port Isaac   77
Rumps Point   *Old School Hotel*   River Lyd
Golden Lion   River Kensey
The Doom Bar   25   81 Greystone Bridge
Quies   Trevose Head   Portquin   Treburley   Milton Abbot
The Bull   Rock   85   Tavistock
21 Padstow   River Camel   *The Royal Inn &*   Horsebridge
The Shipwright Arms   *Horsebridge Brewery*   89
Wadebridge   Bodmin Moor   Gunnislake Dam
Morwellham Quay
Bodmin   River Tamar
Watergate Bay

Harbour Hotel
The Goose   Newquay   C O R N W A L L
Kelsey Head   Zoo   Bugle   River Fowey   Plymouth
Penhale Point   17

Perran Beach
Perranporth   St. Austell
St. Agnes Head   Portwrinkle
Porthtowan   4
Portreath   Mevagissey
Gull Rock •   Truro   41 93
Godrevy   Gorran Haven
Island 13   Redruth
St. Ives   Camborne   Gull Rock

Hayle
Penzance   Falmouth   E N G L I S H

Mousehole   C H A N N E L

Land's End   Goonhilly
N

50°N   Cadgwith
Gull Rock   Lizard Point   10 miles

A T L A N T I C

O C E A N

50°40'

50°N

Epic, Over & Out

Preamble

The rabbit hopped out. Confused, he dithered then hopped back. Stu' swerved slightly. My disinterested "What's up?" met with an evasive, "Err, hmm . . . "

I was unaware of a kindly deceit. Legend has it — if a seaman on his way to embarkation sees a rabbit, he must return home or the voyage will be ill-fated. Months later, Stuart came clean about the incident that occurred on an elevated section of the A30 near Hayle.

Awake, but with closed eyes, my tired mind was in overdrive. There was little time and much to worry about.

HEADLANDS and a HIGH FENCE
(St Ives to Newquay)

Dawn was breaking. St Ives was deserted. Tranquillity would remain for several hours. We lifted Epic down from the van, parked near Smeaton's (lighthouse) Pier, and carried her down to the sandy beach outside the harbour. There was little wind and the sea was fairly flat. I raised the mast and hoisted the twin sails which fluttered gently. My heart did likewise while I tried to appear intrepid — tying the oars and rowlocks to the fairlead fixing on the gunwale with long bootlaces. Stuart shared his flask of tea with me. I drank from a plastic, lidded yoghurt container that I had saved and cleaned. The stout wide-based pot with air-tight lid, I knew would come in handy. I hate throwing usable things away. (A screw-top washing-up liquid bottle, my water container for painting trips, was serving me well after fifteen years. Appropriately, it once contained 'eco' friendly liquid.) After I had tied on my deflated life jacket we exchanged low-key farewells.

Enjoying the luxury of a dry launching — thanks to a calm sea and green wellingtons, I pushed Epic into the water. Wavelets ran over the sand as 'scene one' ended quietly. My haulier headed to the south coast, and I into the Atlantic Ocean.

Stuart had arrived, with roof-racked van, at my home in Mevagissey before 3:00am. Two and a half hours earlier, after several days of adverse forecasts, there was confirmation over the airways of imminent favourable weather. Though early to bed, I had not slept. The commencement of the third part of my trip round Cornwall and the underlying worry that it may not all be plain sailing, kept me awake. Daytime was fine — with thoughts of sunshine and balmy breezes I was raring to go. Night-time triggered doom-laden imaginings when I wished for winds too strong to take Epic on the Ocean. June 28th — no reprieve. The stubborn stillness of the unruffled darkness prevented windy excuses. My goose was in the oven.

The driver had no reason to be chirpy — it was pre-dawn and he was dropping me off on his way to work. The sadistic timing of our journey, due to the tides, would make him many hours early. On a Gorran Haven to Falmouth trip, particularly in the dark, St Ives is an unrewarding diversion. It is also four times further. I should have tried to be sociable but found it difficult to chat.

At 5:25, with a gentle breeze over the starboard quarter, I sailed towards Godrevy Lighthouse. The red jib and the blue Bosun (a cut down jib from a Bosun dinghy, used as a mainsail) eased me away from St Ives. The sky was clear save for hazy sunrise pink, low down, above the mainland to the east. The church, lighthouses and a ribbon of patchwork buildings soon coalesced. The preparation and organization was over. I was free. After twenty minutes the sun rose over Godrevy Island. It was good to be back.

Anna Hill still captained the shipping forecast. Land's End is the centre of four shipping areas. Half an hour into the voyage Anna gave, 'Southerly, four to five, occasionally six.' That was for Sole. Plymouth was better, '. . . three to four, veering westerly, five later.' It was ominously calm at the time. The wind, far from increasing died down and I was rowing by the time I made my approach to the gap between the lighthouse and Godrevy Point at 6:45am.

The tide took Epic swiftly into the channel. One minute I was conveyed on smooth velvety sea, the next I was wildly manipulating the oars to gain purchase as Epic rattled around on short steep waves. Aggressive patches of white water suggested submerged rocks. There was a confused minute of pitching and hull banging, then calm again. I was worried for a while. It was all so sudden.

The octagonal white lighthouse stood solidly in a walled garden with small stone buildings. It would make a peaceful home. Visitors would have to be serious. Fair-weather landing was/is obviously possible; for lighthouse keepers, who no longer keep, must have gained access.

I rowed for a further two miles then row-sailed (using one oar) with the red jib set till 8:00, when I set both sails. The tides were quite swift and by 8:30 Portreath was abeam. With a fresh offshore beam breeze stretching my little sails I was encouraged to head on towards Newquay. Over the next five hours I enjoyed exhilarating sailing. As the wind gradually increased I got used to easing the Bosun sheet when the pressure brought the gunwale to the sea. The relatively flat sea, due to the offshore wind, gave me an easy passage till a near tipping off Perranporth. It is the headlands that cause most difficulties. Another close shave off St Agnes hastened me to reef the main (wrap the Bosun once round the mast).

Once past Perran Beach there were six rocky headlands to negotiate before reaching Newquay Harbour. My course, for interest and protection from the wind, took me inside the off-lying islets at Penhale Point and Kelsey Head. Penhale has Gull Rocks to seaward; no surprise there. Gull Rocks abound round Cornwall, and other coastlines too I suppose. Kelsey has The Chick, which is bigger than the little island off the penultimate promontory, Pentire Point East, which boasts The Goose.

The tide was increasingly against me so wind power was essential. The waters inside the first 'bird islands' gave me a rough ride. I chickened out at The Goose and bashed on outside in choppy waters towards the final obstruction, Towan Head. That two mile slog off Fistral Beach was quite trying, for the south-east wind was very strong, forcing me to take in the Bosun. Trying to restrain the flapping sail and capture the halyard before it flew from the mast-head, while steering, caused some huffing and tangling. The adverse tide created little waves that slowed Epic and forced me to continually play the tiller to maintain the heading. Perhaps play is too delicate a word, it was hardly fine tuning.

GODREVY LIGHTHOUSE

'The tide took Epic swiftly into the channel.'

13

With great relief, at 1:45am, I passed Towan Head and clawed down the remaining sail. It was not too easy when lying and trying to keep weight aft. The wide flat bottom of the Mirror dinghy rapidly narrows as it folds round to meet the flat triangular bow, making the boat decidedly unstable if weight is transferred forward. I had to rush to save myself being blown out to sea and in the confusion the red jib went overboard. With the wet sail bundled in the bottom of the boat I spent a strength-sapping fifteen minutes rowing to Newquay Harbour. With normal rowing I made no headway and had to up the tempo and forgo listening to the shipping forecast. That final mile took a great deal of effort — more than I would have wished, but I was delighted to have travelled so far along the north coast of Cornwall.

Epic grounded on the flat sand just inside the harbour entrance. All was quiet. Big waves crashed periodically onto the beach, past the harbour, where squealing bathers were entertained by the tumbling surf.

Within twenty minutes of stepping onto the firm sand, while enjoying the windless calm inside the protective harbour walls, I was greeted by a victual-bearing Ann. Dennis, the other half of the couple, had purchased from me an old seventeen foot GRP and plywood sailing cruiser named Ant. That was some twenty years before. We had kept in touch and fortunately for me, on their return from Australia, they had settled in Newquay. An ice-cool Fosters was immediately and lovingly analysed by my grateful throat. Though I had not expected to arrive that day, Ann had cast an eye over the harbour when passing and chanced to notice the little white dinghy. In addition to the canned nectar I was 'hampered' with crisps, bananas, a bottle of water and a large fruit-cake. A summertime Christmas — quite Antipodean.

Having arranged to meet for a drink on the veranda of the Harbour Hotel in the evening, I was left to tidy Epic and report to the Harbourmaster. In a couple of hours I would be able to float Epic, as the tide came in, towards the top of the harbour beach where a stone bollard protruded from the sand. My dinghy would be safe overnight as part of a running-line, passing from the bow, round the bollard, back past Epic and through a link in one of the many mooring chains that lay on the harbour bed. I did not realize at the time, how safe.

Between 5:00 and 7:00, with my charge on a longline, I periodically moved the dinghy up towards the mooring point. It was a most frustrating chore for the Ireland v Norway World Cup Match was being televised and was three-quarters the way through before tethering was complete. No goals had been scored when I sat down with my celebration cut-price pint of Guinness. Unfortunately, nil all was the final score and Ireland was out of the competition.

The earlier shipping forecast (17:50) had included '. . . south south-west five to six; rain, drizzle . . .' The 'five to six' was not the time (although it was) but an over-strong wind. That, and the predicted precipitation, plus the football result, dampened my spirits a little.

After a therapeutic pint, drizzle drove us from the balcony. In a chill wet wind we walked down to the harbour to collect my waterproofs. From the quay-side we viewed Epic, safely afloat. Of the bollard there was no sign — it was totally submerged. Earlier, clandestine thoughts had formed when I was told the harbour was a no go area overnight. During the trips I had always stayed on or close by Epic at night. I was quite prepared to hang around for a few hours — till I could collect my wet-weather clothing. Later, when all was quiet, I could sneak back to the boat.

"You must come back. We have a spare bed. You'll get soaked."

"I always stay with Epic."

My proposed action did not impress my psychologist friends. The more I fought my case, the more lunatic I appeared.

"We would not be happy . . ."

I would not have been wholly happy either. The spirit of the voyage would be broken if I accepted the kind offer; but on the other hand I did not want them to feel responsible for a soggy sailor. Of course a warm bed did not enter the equation. I talked my conscience round later.

Before I slept I received an encouraging '. . . south-west four to five, becoming southerly three later'. I slept well but dreamt of roaring animals. Perhaps it was the sound-track accompanying the subconscious memories of my wild ride to Newquay. My dream had seemed real so that in the morning, hoping I was talking to the man and not the psychologist, I asked Dennis if he had heard anything unusual during the night. Animal noises are quite usual in that neighbourhood. A lion enclosure did not spring to mind when a saw a higher than normal fence on my arrival. My hosts' garden, I assumed, abutted the peaceful countryside. It is relatively peaceful living next door to a zoo — roaring lions being preferable to roaring traffic.

GUDGEONS, PINTLES and NOODLES
(Newquay to Padstow)

Dennis gave me a lift to the harbour at 9:00am. There I visited Les, the harbour master, who was most helpful. I did not relate the sunken bollard saga which led to my restful safari. Charts were studied and fishermen quizzed. The consensus was that the wind might moderate sufficiently. Les would tune into the professional shipping forecast for me at 13:40 BST and I would check the 'non-professional' one at five to two. If conditions and the forecasts seemed suitable I would set sail at 4:00ish.

Powerful surges pounded the lower wall and I wondered when the 'southerly three' would arrive. I was relaxing in the sunshine at the top of stone steps on the seaward side of the harbour. Had I not completed what was for Epic a long passage (in excess of 25 miles) the previous day, I would have felt even more a fraud. There I was, lounging around in a holiday resort after a mollycoddled night, and just one day into the voyage. The remainder of the Atlantic coastline beckoned, and my impatience to be on the move took the edge off what could have been a more enjoyable interlude.

On the horizon, a mile off Trevose Head, I saw three small islets (there are more). I was eager to take a closer look but had to be patient and wait to see if conditions improved before making a dash for Padstow — seventeen miles away. As the harbour emptied, a couple of fishing boats set off to sea leaving a free harbour wall. I tied alongside, close to the entrance, in order to be afloat at low tide.

To kill time, for I felt too anxious to paint, I took a stroll along the beautiful golden sands of Watergate Beach. I passed by Sea World where one can walk through a glass tunnel beneath swimming fish, including some shark-like specimens. There is a shallow pool, the sandy bottom of which turns out to be carpeted with huge rays and other flat-fish. To add authenticity there lies, submerged in the pool, a wrecked boat which turns out to be the remains of a Mirror dinghy that met its end off Newquay. With my Watergate investigations completed I returned to watch over Epic.

Two hours after the lunch time '. . . southerly, three to four . . .' forecast, I put my life jacket on and rowed away from Newquay Harbour. It was very windy but the sea had flattened considerably. I hoisted the red jib which I had attached to the forestay while still in harbour, unwrapped the Bosun from the mast and hastened away towards the Quies (the previously mentioned islets). After a mile or so, when I had left the protection of Towan Head and the other Newquay headlands, large swells became apparent. The whole sea surface was bedecked with little waves which gave the crests of swells sinister serrations. The conditions did not bother me too much for I was going the weather way. The waves overtook me slowly and rocked me onwards.

NEWQUAY HARBOUR

'Two hours after the lunchtime ' . . . southerly, three to four . . . ' forecast, I put my life jacket on and rowed away from Newquay Harbour.'

As I approached Trevose Head I aimed for a small rock, The Bull (off Dinas Head), less than a quarter of a mile offshore. A little under ten miles had been covered in two hours forty five minutes. At times just the summit of The Bull, looking black and shark-fin-like, would show and then it would be lost to view along with the headland. It was how I imagined being in mid Atlantic would feel. The shallowing sea around The Bull caused the swells to become steeper with breaking tops. Not wishing to push my luck I set a course outside the islet. I soon found unpredictable, confused waves, steeper and much closer together. All went well till in an attempt to avoid a small portion of ocean that came on board, I rapidly stood up — more of a crouch really. The manoeuvre courted near disaster. When making my foolish stand I accidentally lifted off the tiller and rudder. In less time than it takes to say 'aaaghhh' I was lying prone with my feet thrust against the dinghy-sides and my elbows locked over the transom. Vice-like I grasped the rudder stock and thrust its pintles into the gudgeons. I need not have known that the pins on the rudder were called pintles, or the eyes on the back of Epic were gudgeons, to know that within seconds they had to be reunited. To be out of control in that situation would be an event of short duration. Those of you who have dinghy sailed will know how difficult it is attaching a rudder while afloat. The sea steers the blade till luck lends a hand and allows docking. For rapid repositioning one needs special stimulation — a rush of adrenalin released by acute fear will do the trick.

The Bull rapidly receded; so did the angry waves as I bore right, round the white lighthouse of Trevose. I was in the lee and headed towards Pentire Point, five miles away, though I would take another right hander before then and head up the River Camel.

An evening calm was setting in. Epic glided past Trevone, a good mile offshore. Standing to steer, I attempted to dry my jeans in the fading sunshine. The setting sun lessened the chill of an uncomfortable backside and cast the sailor's shadow on the red sail — how poetic. My earlier cavorting had not saved me from a slight sluicing.

The faceted, peaked waves held an austere grandeur as they ambled eastward. They were no longer aggressive. Their dark side was caused by the low sun angle and their height was exaggerated by my low eye-level — viewing the peaks against the sky. The helpful light airs ceased in the failing light as I turned south, round Stepper Point, into the estuary. It was nine o'clock. Darkness fell as I rowed the two miles up to Padstow. I soon passed over The Doom Bar, tamed by the high tide, the last of which helped me a little against the adverse light breeze. After a mile I came upon a pack of moored, silhouetted boats. With frequent glances over my shoulder I steered between the various pleasure-craft and at 10:30, high tide, was off the open harbour entrance. I did not enter, for I wished to leave in the early hours when the lock-gates would be closed.

Alongside the inner wall of the outer basin, close by the harbour entrance, I temporarily hitched Epic to an iron ladder while I tied ropes to bow and stern. Having clambered up the ladder with my bundles of ropes I secured the bow line to a huge iron ring on the quay. When tying on my extra long stern line I fed the free end down into the boat. The line seemed to have mysteriously lengthened. The end that should have been attached to Epic came to hand with a small galvanized eye fitting with two rusted screw stumps. If you could choose a time for a sheet lead to come adrift that was it — in a harbour with one line already secured. It could have happened off Trevose Head, with the rudder off.

At the harbour office I filled in an entry form. I did not know the gross tonnage but knew the length of the vessel and the crew's full name. For a modest fee I purchased a card that gained entrance to a shower block at the other side of the harbour. The official said I could sleep there if I wished. It was a kind thought — such hospitality again. I thanked him but said I would be sleeping on board.

Time, in respect of Padstow night-life, was at a premium. I hastened into the village and soon chanced upon the eminently sociable, London Inn. After a pleasant, though rather too swift an interlude and pint of Guinness, I nipped into a handy Chinese take-away. Privately and in comforting darkness I dined on board, doing justice to a tasty hot supper. *'Heaven',* I noted in my log book after chasing the last slippery noodle round the tinfoil tray.

To the harbourmaster I had explained my need to be off before low water — to take an eastward ride with the tide. Low tide which was only six hours away would leave Epic mud-bound if I did not move her. At the steps opposite, at the estuary end of the quay, I would still be afloat at departure time.

After my midnight feast, in a state of utter contentment, I ambled round the harbour to the well appointed facility and showered. It was quite cosy but I did not think for a second of spending another night in warm comfort. I did think how pleasant it would be though.

Back at my berth (this is not a flashback) I carefully lowered my mooring lines into Epic as I climbed down the ladder, making sure they would not go overboard. Being squeaky-clean and salt-free I had no wish to share my limited space with a load of wet rope. I rowed over to my night station and fixed lines that could be cast off without my leaving the boat; for I was sure there would be drifts of glutinous mud around the lower steps when I wished to leave. Relocated, I arranged my dry sleeping bag on the picnic-box, thwart and centre-board, then, metaphorically speaking, drifted off. All had been plain sailing since my fright off Trevose Head. It was a dry night and my luck seemed to be holding. The last time I slept on board was at Mousehole the previous August, when it rained.

MAGWITCH and THE DOOM BAR
(Padstow to Port Isaac)

It must have been about 1:00am when I entered the bag. Floating about in a little boat, being edged this way and that by the mooring lines, really is most relaxing. The edging stopped. My rest period was over. After two hours of slumber Epic grounded, or 'very sticky muddied'. So far, the harbour officials I encountered seemed to have problems assessing water levels. Was I unlucky with my harbourmasters or did they have a strange sense of humour? There was a moment of hurried action off that flight of extremely muddy steps. I retrieved mooring lines, plopping them on the foredeck — for swilling later. With the spade-ended oar* I set about spooning myself off the mud.

"Wondered what you wus up to." A deep voice came from the darkness at the top of the steps. I detected a vague form and thought of Magwitch. It was as well the tone conveyed no menace, for my escape, had it been necessary, would have been a bit of a long shot. Having extricated Epic from the ooze I rounded the pier-end and tied to a sunken pontoon type structure which gurgled and hissed periodically as it slowly drained.

"It does that sometimes." Magwitch was still there.

I washed my lines and oar in the sea and got back into my bag for a further ten minutes. My rather pointless lie-in was not at all restful. It was not just the hidden eyes; I was also contemplating The Doom Bar.

Around 4:00 an orange dawn was in the making. It was time to leave if I was to exit the Camel before low tide. On my way to the office, to return my shower block pass card, I had a brief chat with the nocturnal one — a net fisherman waiting for low water and the incoming salmon. I phoned the coastguard, informing them of my imminent departure. A short while later an outboard engine coughed into life, heralding the fisherman's departure. At 4:15 I followed, rowing out of the shallow channel that hugged the town-side of the estuary. Many acres of exposed Town Bar sand was to starboard (my left, for my back 'faced' the sea). To the east, in darkness, lay the village of Rock, where incidentally, a pleasant ale called Doom Bar is brewed.

A mile on at Gun Point, the netsman stood silently by his boat as Epic grazed the sand in the shallows and headed onwards, towards The Bar. At first the waves, born between headlands then constricted by shallows, were barely noticeable. As if gentle hands slowly wafted giant silken banners, smooth, silent undulations moved upriver. The incoming tide soon began an eager advance. Small waves formed at the channel edges, the ends flipping onto the sands with a periodic slight 'sssh'. The breaking sections increased in length as the rounded swells grew. In a few minutes Epic no longer lifted over the steepening peaks but pivoted sharply. The breaking waves crashed noisily each side of the estuary. Soon, white water stretched from shore to shore, save for a narrow mid section. I rowed with 'enthusiasm' to pass The Bar before the 'door closed'. With the oar-tips close to tumbling surf I broke out and rowed into relatively calm water.

---

* My oars are non-matching. The spade-ended one is much lighter. The other, a better roller — as you will see.

PADSTOW

'It was time to leave if I was to exit the Camel before low tide.'

Had I forgone my lie-in I may have avoided the bar-roulette. With my pulse-rate returning to normal I hoisted the gib. Inside Stepper Point a motor sailor slowly motored back and forth, waiting for sufficient water to clear The Doom Bar.

The sun came up at 5:30 as I rounded Pentire Point (three miles from Padstow). The seas were largish and lumpy but I was able to catch the shipping forecast. It was slow going as I made my way round Rumps Point to the lee of The Mouls — a small islet another mile on and a quarter-mile offshore. There I downed sail and finished cleaning the boat. Even at that early hour it was hot. Under the clear blue sky I applied sun block and donned my sun-hat. The wind was from the south-east, rather than the forecast '. . . south, three to four'. If the discrepancy had been clockwise (veered instead of backed) I could have utilised windpower. Instead I positioned the oars in the rowlocks and pulled to the east, towards Port Isaac.

'7:35 Wind calmer — perhaps in lee of Portquin — Stop breakfast . . .' The tide at last was becoming favourable and I '. . . drift right way'. Gently rocking across Portquin Bay towards Kellan Head, which guarded the extremely-difficult-to-spot Portquin channel, I munched on Ann's cherry and walnut cake and sipped cool orange juice. Location can be an important ingredient. Interludes of such perfection are rare. Was there ever a better breakfast? How pleasurable it was to drift on the sun-drenched ocean which was in such benevolent mood. The awe-inspiring seascape was unadulterated, except for a plywood dinghy, a fruit-cake, etc.

A secret harbour is hard to resist. The little inlet looked so inviting on the OS (Ordnance Survey) map that I had to investigate. Just off the entrance lie the Cow & Calf — small, low lying rocky obstructions that must have claimed a great deal of shipping when Portquin was a commercial harbour. Other submerged formations left confusions of swirling water just beyond the rocks towards the channel entrance. I held station for a while, to plot a safe passage, then gingerly rode the swells between the tumbling surf. Inside all was serene and grandly empty. Not a place for shouting, or outboards. A sign by the Cow & Calf suggesting 'by appointment only' would not have seemed out of place.

The steep cliffs and precipitous grassy sides to the quarter-mile long 'mini-fiord' precluded all human interference at the waterside till the hamlet-end was reached. There, ten or so dwellings huddled snugly. Set back, high in the centre of the undulating grassy top of Doyden Point (on the western side of the inlet) stands Doydon Castle. Just the top of a crenellated tower seems to be visible — but that is all there is. It was built in the early eighteen hundreds for 'recreational purposes' — how discreet. As I made my way down the channel I noticed a figure in red standing on the slip at the far end. There was no need to intrude. In any case there was sure to be a bit of ocean motion swilling the slip. At 8:30 I raised the Bosun and headed seawards.

Propelled by sail and oar, Epic lolloped along to Port Isaac — arriving at 10:20am. Port Isaac harbourside was not as tightly packed with buildings as would be the less exposed south coast harbours. It has a large harbour-pool but is not overburdened with boats and moorings. Port Isaac's north facing aspect would account for that. The long mooring chains suggest a powerful surge is not uncommon. It was a surprise to find the harbour was almost deserted. Getting up so early had put me in p.m. mode. There was still an hour before high-water but I decided not to drag Epic higher up the beach, for apart from the sandy patch where I landed, it was quite stony. The time would soon arrive when my respect for the finish on my freshly painted white dinghy would diminish. Epic took several bursts of sandy water up the centre-board case. ' — *I hate that!!*' I wrote, as if it were someone-else's fault. It was time to relax. 'Boat lag' was setting in.

Overlooking the harbour, from the Golden Lion, I looked down at Epic. The smallness of my boat always surprised me. It was my world for many hours, yet I was unaware of confinement. There was never a dull moment for I was always heading towards new experiences on waters new to me. I was the sole customer in the pub and was treated royally. It was no trouble to provide tea, which I consumed copiously.

Two hours after arriving, one of the few people on the beach helped me carry Epic down to the receding sea. Thinking positively, in order to be able to continue the voyage without delay if conditions allowed, I rowed out to the east harbour wall. Before executing the manoeuvre I consulted a fisherman about my plan. Imagine my surprise when, in close proximity to the wall, I found three metal stanchions occasionally breaking the surface. They were part of 'safety-rails' on steps leading from a mid-tide-level platform. It would have been ironic to have Epic skewered on a safety-rail.

The inner harbour wall sloped out considerably down to the harbour bed and the additional structure made loading and unloading safer and easier at lower tide. To save Epic from severe grating I looped a stern-line over an outer stanchion top and took a mid-gunwale line along towards the harbour entrance. The arrangement unfortunately did not prevent a periodic grinding on the barnacled wall. Fenders were needed which called for a sacrifice. (I was without live chickens, which would have sunk in any case.) My half surfboard/seat I broke into four pieces. The extremely buoyant polystyrene, with thick loops of cord passing through well away from the edges, kept the barnacles at bay. The tethered jetsam performed with distinction and my fear that the line would pull through the makeshift fenders proved unfounded.

Captain's log, 4:30pm. '*Still V windy — lot of seahorses seems to be from the north . . .*' I had phoned Falmouth coastguard at 3:00 to say I would carry on if the wind moderated and was favourable. I received their forecast ' . . . variable, two to three becoming easterly three'. The 'variable' would have been acceptable but I was experiencing what seemed like a northerly five, blowing straight into the harbour. I would have liked to carry on — using two tides in one day. There were only two or three legs left before I would run out of Cornwall, so that may have been my last chance. '*I'll wait till 5:30 . . .*' — Captain's log, 4:35.

23

After a walk, and fish'n'chips on the cliffs, the deadline arrived. No change. I arranged with John, the Harbourmaster, to leave Epic on the hard at the top of the beach. A voyage-abort call to the coastguard followed. Finally I phoned Julia, asking if I and my gear could be picked up. With at least an hour to kill I wandered back up the hill to the Old School Hotel. I was feeling stiff of back, and my face was sunburned and felt red (it was). My hand-backs were also burned, and my palms oar-blistered. A few more days of acclimatisation would have hardened me off. I was peeved at the postponement. On my trip round Cornwall the weather had allowed no more than four days without disruption, and I had hoped to 'do the North Coast' without adjournment. A feeling of slight depression, which had nothing to do with my clapped-out state, had set in.

On the Hotel terrace it was again tea-time. Epic, I could see, was acquitting herself well against the harbour wall. *'Suddenly looked on the bright side.'* The snippet, written at the tea-table, continued. *'Good distance. Have just phoned for a lift. Productive 3 days . . .'* My outlook changes with the wind.

Later, myself and many others were being entertained down at the harbour beach by a silver band. Port Isaac was in party mood. My attention was not wholly captured for I realised Epic could be cut off by the rising tide. I made my way along the rudimentary, cliff hugging causeway that was being lapped by the rising tide. Aboard Epic I disassembled my fenders, cast off and rowed towards boats moored mid-harbour, intending to hitch alongside one. A shout from Neil rendered that manoeuvre unnecessary. After a couple more pulls on the oars, Epic glided onto the beach. In no time at all the dinghy was chocked-up beyond the high-water mark and mast and oars tied on top of the Fiesta. In no time plus ten minutes, my impromptu pick-up team, Neil and his brother-in-law Dave, joined me in the Golden Lion. We supped our pints as the band marched past the window booming out the Flora Dance.

PORT ISAAC

'I arranged with John, the Harbourmaster, to leave Epic on the hard at the top of the beach.'

"WE CAN'T FORCE YOU"
(Port Isaac to Boscastle)

Days, along with windy forecasts, passed. Noon, Sunday 10th July, looked promising, but not quite enough — *'Lundy S 4 5 Dec 3, rain in W'* (It was not December 3rd, Dec = decreasing). The next day, Neil and I sat outside The Shipwright Arms above Port Isaac, ready for the shipping forecast. Radio reception was impossible down by the harbour. *'1:55 pm, S bec. var. 3 4 bec W'* (becoming variable). I would have been happy to cast my caution at the prescribed wind, but as it was blowing freshly from the north I was in two minds. When viewed from that high vantage point the sea looked deceptively flat, so I decided to have a go. Neil and I had endured a journey of jams. He would have the same on his return, whereas I was unlikely to meet a single craft on my way to Boscastle.

At 3:10 I rowed out of Port Isaac and into the wind. I set both sails and added to progress, using one or other oar, for an hour. The wind was always blowing from Tintagel Head — situated six miles north, north-east of Port Isaac. By a visual check on the position of the islands to the west, just off Rumps Point, I was not making enough progress northwards. My heading with both sails set was too far off the wind so I pulled down the jib, securing it with a rubber shock-cord. With the Bosun set and my right hand oar doing overtime I made reasonable progress, though still heading out to sea rather too much. (With both sails set not enough attention can be given to rowing.)

I knew it would not be easy to beat the tide before nightfall but was confident of rounding the historic headland of Tintagel and finding, three miles further on, the hidden harbour of Boscastle. To pass between towering cliffs and enter the small, rugged and mysterious harbour of Boscastle, situated at the end of a narrow channel, was my most eagerly awaited moment of the trip. I had visions of completing a solitary passage along that romantic coastline; then spending a night lost in the solitude of a legendary hideaway. It was also well on my way to Devon.

At 6:00, I was about a mile or so offshore and judging my progress against another Gull Rock — a third of a mile off Trebarwith Strand and two thirds the distance towards the headland. Heading up the coast in my general direction I detected a small, engine powered boat. The distraction, as the craft made good time bouncing over the waves, was quite welcome for I had seen practically no other boats at sea on the north coast section of the voyage. It seemed too small to be a real boat at first; then I saw three people on board. They were heading my way. When fifty yards away I realised my visitors, dressed alike in yellow oilskins and red life jackets, were lifeboat-men. As they slowed down I read the RNLI on the bow of the rubber boat. It was only at that moment, I realised with dread that I was the reason for their mission. As the grey and orange boat bumped against Epic I felt really bad. I knew they had come to rescue me. They did not know that I did not want to be rescued. It is not like refusing a lift from a passing car. Those dedicated men had received a call, had launched a boat, had travelled four miles and were 'going' to tow me back to Port Isaac.

That conversation off Trebarwith Strand was difficult for me. For the life-saving crew to allow a 'kamikaze' mission was out of the question. Without offending I had to justify my actions. My qualification — having got so far unaided, was not necessarily sufficient justification. Perhaps I was a lucky mariner. They did not want me to carry on, towards dusk and dangerous headlands. It would involve several hours of rowing and they obviously were not to know if I had the strength for the undertaking. It would not be straightforward rowing — there would be constant manipulation of the oars to counteract the motion of the confused seas round the headlands and progress would be slow. Doing their best to dissuade me, they said I did not have time to row to Boscastle before nightfall. I was about to succumb, 'advantage against', when their "... we can't force you . . ." reversed the balance. 'Match point', but it was a close call. It was as well no vote was taken.

The 'action men' did not return to base but roared off, as if let out to play, to find out what conditions were like 'round the corner'. They seemed to be enjoying themselves, which made me feel a lot better. I was on my best behaviour, efficiently plying the oars with gusto, when they returned fifteen minutes later. Meanwhile, there had been communication with Falmouth Coastguard who asked the lifeboat-men to keep me company till I had rounded Tintagel Head. The hour it took to reach, then to round the headland was slightly stressful. Not wishing to keep my escorts waiting I put extra effort into rowing, wondering if I could keep up the pace. It was agreeable to chat with the crew from time to time and they assured me it was no trouble to be out on such a fine evening. Occasionally they zipped off to investigate caves, which when flooded by rising swells created huge plumes of surf that dwarfed their lifeboat. To see the small inflatable at the foot of the towering cliffs gave me a better idea of the scale of my surroundings, and the smallness of Epic.

Before turning back to Port Isaac the crew described the markers of the concealed entrance. On the high promontory to the west of the channel stands a square, white look-out resembling a tiny fort, and on the other side is a mast-aerial. With their task completed the lifeboat-men departed.

I had my voyage back and checked my exact location against OS 200. A headland named Willapark, a mile on from Tintagel Head, was the final feature on the map. On the adjoining map, OS 190, there is another headland of a similar size, just two miles further on — this is also named Willapark. Both have traces of Iron Age fortifications. Fortunately, the first does not have a mini-fort/lookout. Even Gull Rocks are not that close together.

When three men in a grey and red inflatable raced up from the west I could have been forgiven for thinking that the area possessed a duplication phenomenon — a variation on the Bermuda Triangle.

"Falmouth Coastguard have asked us to escort you to Boscastle." The boys were back.

Chaperoned again, I battled on. The RNLI service, which 'adopted' me for so long, really is a tremendous organisation. They are on call, not just on fine evenings in the summer but throughout the wild winter months when conditions are very unpleasant and frightening. Please give generously.

With the huge King Arthur's Castle Hotel making frequent appearances between the grassy-topped headlands I progressed slowly towards Boscastle. The hotel was built about seven hundred years after the castle, of which very little remains. I did not notice the castle as I passed by. It blends well with the landscape, unlike the hotel.

It was after 8:30 when we passed between the craggy Meachard islet (two to three hundred yards along) and the second Willapark headland and into the harbour channel. The crew advised me to keep a central course. Back-wash created a great deal of motion in the confined space which made for uneasy rowing. The sound of the seas in that craggy amphitheatre scored a memorable finale to an unusual leg of the voyage. From the steep, ferny, gorsey, heathery hillside that overlooked the channel, a few small groups of holiday-makers watched the end of the show. There were no credits to say that the one in the little white boat would rather have come quietly, on his own. I waved goodbye to the lifeboatmen and wondered what they were saying about their odd evening and 'escortee' as they powered back to Port Isaac.

In calm water I temporarily tied Epic against the inside of the inner harbour wall. It was 8:45. With relief I laid the oars along the gunwales and climbed onto the steep, narrow stone slip. Oddly, I was not unduly tired after my exertions; but I was relieved to relax mentally. I no longer had to concern myself with Falmouth Coastguard or three men in a boat. Once I had upped the tempo after 'forming convoy' I seemed to lock into automatic row mode. I was still able to soak up the peaceful surroundings but was rather self-conscious and not wholly at ease. Sometimes it is better to arrive than to travel.

On warm windless days Boscastle is a cosy little harbour. During winter storms it would be bleak indeed — not even overlooked by the hamlet which nestles in relative safety a couple of hundred yards back. Through the lower village and down into the narrow harbour runs the small River Valency.

The evening was becoming a touch grey and there was a feeling of dampness in the air. In a cottage on the other side of the rushing river I found Fred the Harbourmaster and paid my 'Dinghy overnight stay' fee. I made a couple of phone calls on my way to the Cobweb Inn. A swift pint of mild was followed by a stroll back to the harbour with a beef-burger in hand — a savoury to savour. I was anxious to moor Epic a little upstream from the fishing boats, out of the way of any morning manoeuvring. It was prudent to move to an overnight parking position while there was plenty of water, and in case I got caught in the Cobweb. The boats, moored bow to quay with chains round sturdy wooden bollards, numbered eleven and were fifteen to twenty-five feet in length. Most were open craft powered by outboards. All are taken out of the water for the winter.

Before midnight I lay down in/on Epic. I was excited at the prospect of making my way out of that crazy sanctuary and completing my journey round the Cornish coastline. The temperature eased down to 'uncomfortable' and I slipped into my sleeping bag. Later a light drizzle descended. Accustomed as I was, I drew on my orange plastic survival bag and happily perspired into the night; spirit undampened.

BOSCASTLE

'On warm windless days Boscastle is a cosy little harbour.'

"DON'T GO"
(Boscastle to Bude)

The harbour emptied as I steamed in my bag. After grounding for a couple of hours in the drizzly darkness, Epic floated in the new day. A duck-enriched dawn began just after 4:00. The frenetic dabbling of the salt-water ducks was due to the rushing Valency River, racing over the slippery, water-worn stones. The idyll remained, despite the sound of scouring water and agitated quacks. I was content to observe and relax in the pleasant lull. While peeling my breakfast I noticed the banana-skin exactly matched my oilskin. At 5:15, with optimism — for the hill-tops were shrouded in mist, I hoisted my royal blue sleeping-bag to dry. The modest scale of the enterprise was emphasized when I realized that the unzipped bag was much larger than the Bosun. Later in the day I would make observations of greater consequence.

Most of the boats were afloat. A slight swell ran in behind them causing a little motion. To evaluate sea conditions I took a walk out to the end of the promontory, Willapark No 2. The conflict of sea against cliff produced a great deal of noise from the channel and island as on the previous evening. As I progressed upwards, the sea's motion appeared less obvious and I imagined myself rowing out through the skeins of white. My eagerness should have been tempered, for I knew the cause of that patterning. There were two shipping forecasts before I would know if it was safe to set out for Bude. Patience was required.

I brushed on upwards through the ferns. Over the hill, across the valley, the sun's glare was diffused by the expanding mist that seeped seawards between the hills. Reclining in the heather and ferns and soft grass — the shiny round-stemmed type, I continued my breakfast. The lump, I knew started life as ham, chutney and lettuce sandwiches. (I had experienced something similar after my arrival at Cadgwith a year earlier.) As before, the battered and compressed presentation did nothing to diminish my appetite. Dining was disrupted and my spirit dipped a little after the shipping forecast. 'Veering . . . three to four; occasional rain or drizzle.' An onshore force four at Bude was too much for my little boat; but there was plenty of time for moderation.

While taking note of 'Occasional rain in Sole . . .' I noticed that the fog/cloud out to sea between the headlands was clearing, revealing a soft blue sky. I continued munching my distressed sandwich. By 6:30 I was reclining on an exposed slab of rock on the cliff edge. Close by was the lookout, which I drew in the logbook. Afterwards I made a sketch of the headlands that I hoped I would soon sail round. An ominous bank of cloud developed out to sea. As I shaded the feature it grew and spread landwards. *'7:15 Fog from land & sea meet. Sun obscured. Vis.2 1/2 mls.'* There was plenty of time for visibility to return. I set off to walk round the village.

After a climb up to higher Boscastle I had the pleasure of visiting an art gallery. There was plenty of time for me to paint and rich subject matter on hand, but I could not settle and muster the necessary concentration. My mind was engaged in running through my forthcoming push towards Devon — out through the channel and along the coastline to Bude. I became increasingly worried about the procedure as time passed. I ambled round for a short while, then to conserve energy, made my way back down the hill. Not far from the harbour I chanced upon the Toby Jug Restaurant where I enjoyed a second breakfast. I received more than my requested much mushroomed and tomato'd pieces of toast. It was suggested I have a word with a local seaman who worked out of Boscastle. The proprietor recommended I make haste to the harbour from where Ken was preparing to set out.

Presently I was engaged in a short, shouted conversation with the obliging skipper who was on board 'Pengenna'. After introducing myself and stating my destination. I gave the forecast wind direction and strength. The oracle said "Don't go". Until nearing high-water a Bude landing is a beach landing and not safe for boats even in a moderate onshore wind. The sensible course of action has been given loud and clear — an unequivocal, not yet. I should have been delighted with my reprieve but foolishly thought I could just pop out into the Atlantic Ocean and if the lunch-time forecast showed no improvement, just pop back.

Again, bedevilled by the lure of adventure, I had been tempted to ignore prudence and continue the voyage. This strange quirk acts against my better judgement. A self-hypnosis just happens. While things were going well I enjoyed my immortality.

I informed Falmouth Coastguard of my intentions and at 11:25 cast off. Gripping the oars tightly, I tentatively rocked out of the channel. Taking my time, for low water was over two hours away, I made my way between the Meachard and Penhally Point, away from the sounding surf and out to sea. A short distance away from the cliffs the ocean was almost flat. Though slightly overcast, the clouds were high-ish, except over the land where change seemed possible.

In a little while a gentle wind breezed Epic Budewards. At noon, with the Bosun raised against the mast and poled out with the boat-hook and the jib delicately pulling on the forestay, Epic eased north-eastwards. At that time it was still a simple row back to Boscastle. Sometime in the next hour or so I was committed — there would be great danger in trying to beat my way back. At the first and biggest headland, Cambeak on the southern side of Crackington Haven, the power of the ocean became apparent. At 1:30 I noticed, *'Big swells & crashing waves off before Crack'*. Fooled by the sea's lethargic state I had allowed Epic too close to the shore. On a steep onrushing slope, Epic was pushed sideways for a few seconds. A hundred yards further in, a previous swell was turning over and thundering against the jutting dark cliffs.

A simple line drawing in the log-book reminds me of the beginnings of an uneasy feeling that grew over the next few hours. After that worrying moment I drew, in simplified form, my dinghy on the steep landward side of a long swell. Not wishing to be caught out by such sneaky predators I eased Epic further offshore.

Captain's log, *'1:40 Black sk all across. Bos. lost. Ominous calm. Ghosting — poled out Bosun. Must get Ship/f.cast'*. That forecast was virtually the same as the previous one. The only difference being that rain and drizzle were no longer occasional.

At 3:00 the breeze almost deserted me and I did a spell of row/sailing with the sails boomed out with oar and boathook. Not long after, the wind picked up and I made good progress for half an hour. Exhilarated, I stood up and held on to the mast for a few minutes. The dinghy did seem small then — a bit like a slow-motion wind-surfer. Wind-strength increased and games were over. Off Dizzard Point (well over half way) and other nearby outcrops there were breaking seas. By the time I was abeam Millook Haven, a mile on, I was frightened — not by the threatening conditions, which I was getting used to, but by being propelled at too great a speed towards a destination I knew to be inaccessible at that time of tide. Dawdling along had suited me fine. Epic's sudden acceleration during that irresponsible journey to Bude caused me great anxiety. I dreaded the thought of arriving in bad weather and not being able to land because of the surf. Two hours later there would have been sufficient depth of water to allow Epic to round the breakwater and find shelter.

Mist often shrouded the cliff-tops. At times it seemed to brighten and then all land would be obscured, save for a darker shape of an outcrop or headland. The OS 190 map showed a welcome sandy beach at Widemouth Bay. I thought I saw the location but would not have seen the sand from my low viewpoint. If it was Widemouth it was protected by crashing waves. There was great temptation to head in and hope for a safe landing beyond the surf, for I wanted to end the ordeal. With the thought that I might miss Bude preying on my mind I spent a desperate hour in the mist. What if I were driven further along the Atlantic coast — past Hartland Point and on into the Bristol Channel. My mind was in turmoil. I had to locate Bude — for there was nowhere else to go. OS 190 showed Hartland Quay, twenty miles past Bude and a few miles before Hartland Point. That was a long way and with the onshore wind, suggested little hope. The map indicated a hotel, parking and 'Mus' at Hartland Quay. The 'Mus' I took to be a museum — of shipwrecks, perhaps.

Visibility improved and there was definitely a beach ahead. Was that Widemouth? No, there was a tower on the skyline and a breakwater a few hundred yards ahead. I had found Bude. An hour earlier I had decided, if I found myself off Bude, to head straight in and take my chances. There would be people on the beach even if it was raining. Where there are waves and an accessible beach there are usually surfers.

CAMBEAK - on the way to Bude

'Mist often shrouded the cliff-tops. At times it seemed to brighten and then all land would be obscured . . .'

The emotions experienced in the period that followed were beyond my usual. Though worried, I did not think my life was in danger so I decided not to use my distress flares. It had been comforting to have them with me throughout the trip. Fear had not gone away but I felt a bizarre eagerness to experience the outcome.

In a supercharged state I rushed through the necessary preparations. Approaching Bude, after the long period of anxiety, I felt comparatively composed — I quite impressed myself. I wrapped and tied the Bosun round the mast. (The increased wind strength had forced me to take down the jib half an hour before.) There was no time to close my bulging painting bag into which I had hurriedly pushed the map and logbook. Odds and ends, including the broken polystyrene surfboard — fender bits, I stuffed into the cubbyholes. The lid of the red picnic-box fitted tightly, giving me confidence that the Walkman and camera would be safe in what I imagined to be a thoroughly seaworthy container. The centreboard and the rudder I placed on the stern-seat, having de-shipped them in a frantic trice. For the second time in my life I fully inflated my life jacket. (The previous occasion was off Portwrinkle, three years before, when I was in a similar situation with Epic. At least I knew where I was this second time.)

When I passed by the breakwater, Epic was perhaps two hundred yards out from the beach. Considering it was not sun bathing weather the sands were well dotted with people. With Epic already rising to the swells I increased my row-rate and headed for the breakers. Rowing aggressively, I surfed on a pre-breaker waveface for a couple of seconds. I had watched surfers and suddenly I was one. For a beautiful moment I really thought I could surf onto the beach. Seconds later, boiling froth piled high over the stern and Epic's blunt bow dipped into the surface, tripping my 'surfboard'. When Epic became vertical a great weight of white water descended. Still holding the oars I awaited the engulfing.

Waking, warm and weightless, I became aware of the situation but felt no panic. A pleasant serenity cradled me. 'I was cold before but now I was warm.' I was face down, under water. There was no need to breathe. Time was standing still. For a few moments I felt something round my legs. Eventually I forced my mouth to the air and as I gulped a little, I heard, then saw the next 'avalanche'. I wanted to breathe then, but had to be patient.

I wore a heavy jumper, jeans and green wellingtons. Heading towards Bude I ran through my beaching procedure many times. Removing wellies was a major priority but I somehow forgot in the 'excitement'. When I came out of the second roller I took in a good supply of air. I saw the Mirror riding high on her buoyant side, dragging the mast and drifting onto the beach. My wellingtons made contact with the sand. As I bobbed towards the beach a bronzed life guard on a surfboard paddled up to me and asked if I was alright. I said "Yes thank you."

With the Atlantic lapping about my waist I was acutely aware of gravity and felt extremely heavy. In slow motion, I ponderously headed towards my natural element. Fantastic fortune favoured me at that auspicious moment. To port, close to my thigh, I spotted my grey nylon painting bag. It hovered below the surface in a most surreal manner. The contents seemed to be in place. Again I had the good fortune to be reunited with my cardboard paint-box and brush tube with brushes (circa 1980). Peeping from the open bag, alongside the map, was my precious log/note-book. It was a 'Daliesque' performance — my lifting the bag from the waters, emptying a couple of pints and nonchalantly putting the strap over my shoulder. Normally I would have felt rather self-conscious with my fully inflated life jacket bulging beneath my stretched and dripping jumper and water dribbling from my welly-tops. It was not a normal time. Relief cast aside any embarrassment. Though strained and draining, it was a mightily thankful mariner who walked from the water onto Bude beach.

At first sight Epic seemed in a bad way — resting at a sad one hundred degrees at the tide-line. I thought the mast was broken, but an oar had fixed itself to the mast and shroud, and the boat-hook was attached to the fore-stay. All were tangled in my very long, green mooring rope. Minnie the muscular lifeguard and I righted Epic and the wind pressed her safely against the beach. While I emptied Atlantic from my wellingtons, lifeguards and others collected together my flotsam. Portions of broken polystyrene, with cord attached, flew up the beach. I hated being responsible for such litter. Later (it may have been ten minutes or thirty) the last item to be recovered was returned to Epic. An oar had come adrift and broken away a rowlock housing, sending the small galvanized plate to the bottom of the sea. The bootlaces had not kept the oar and boat together but I was pleased to see they had held the rowlock to the oar. I had conceded very little to Neptune. The rowlock plate was joined by a few pound coins, a small bucket and short lengths of rope. My oilskin must have sunk and drifted off like a yellow skate, never to be seen again. It may have been the jacket that brushed my legs when I was in the water. Perhaps even now, off the coast of Bude, a yellow, handless sleeve beckons from the deep.

Minnie asked if I would like to use the phone in the hut at the top of the beach. My first call was to Falmouth Coastguard, informing them of my arrival — I did not go into details. The second call was to Julia, requesting a lift home and dry clothes.

Back down at the waterline I thanked Minnie and assessed the situation. I released the oar and boathook from the rigging and noticed a bunch of bungy-ties at the masthead. My 'seaworthy' red box turned out to have a cunning, ventilation system. It had stood on the beach for half an hour, innocently protecting two gallons of sea under which soaked my Walkman, camera and numerous other items. The camera was bought because of its 'water resistant' claim. Though fearing malfunction I aimed the severely tested instrument at my gleaming and virtually undamaged Epic.

At 5:15, I took my pen and damp logbook from the soggy painting bag and on the cover noted the estimated time and the date of my capsize — '*4:45 12 July.*' That small task was not too easy for my hands were becoming numb, but I felt the need to take away a physical token of the episode.

For the next two hours I was kept busy leading Epic, at the pace of the incoming tide, up the course of the channel formed by the River Neet as it flowed down the beach to where I had landed (if that is the correct terminology). At the top of the watercourse, which was much too shallow to float Epic, stands a quay wall which leads to the lock gates that hold back the waters of the Bude Canal. There is also a slipway that leads up to a small lifeboat station.

With Epic finally tied up alongside the quay I took the plastic bag containing my clothes round to the front of the lifeboat station. Though sheltered from the chilling wind the location lacked privacy and I was rather exposed as I changed into what dry clothes I had. Fortunately, the heavy-duty bag was tied closed with a cord. My lucky shirt* which was at the top of the bag was a little damp but the rest of my ensemble was perfectly dry. Just to be out of the wind was bliss, but to free myself of sodden wool and heavy, cold clinging denim was sublime. That dry towel held power out of proportion to its function, wondrous though that was. After so much discomfort, cold and wetness, that fluffy talisman marked my changed circumstance. In dryish shirt, shorts and battered old trainers, a transformation took place. From the lee of the lifeboat hut emerged, 'Mirrorman'.

In retrospect, the rejuvenated me may not have been fully 'compos mentis'. A wet person, however grateful to be alive, should not have spent a couple of chilling hours on a windy beach — he would have sought help to carry the dinghy above the high-water line. But then, a totally sane person would not have left Boscastle or even St Ives.

Neil had again been pressed into taxi service and duly arrived in his soft-topped motorcar. My intention was to take Epic home for repairs but the convertible forced a change of plan. While I had been dismasting and unloading Epic, two of the lifeboat crew arrived at the hut. Noticing the open front doors I entered. It would be in order to leave Epic alongside the hut for a day or two and no trouble to leave the mast, oars and a few other items inside. While I was filling in the background that led to my request for storage, one of the men noticed a large lump on my right temple. My hair had previously concealed the disfigurement. Being concerned with the well-being of others, the lifeboat-men suggested we hang on a moment — to await the arrival of their medic-man. Though I felt fine and wanted to go home (it had been a long day) I agreed to have my head seen to.

* *The shirt front retained faint marks — the washed out remains of oil staining 'acquired' after my lucky landing at Portwrinkle.*

BUDE

'At the top of the watercourse . . . stands a quay wall which leads to the lock gates . . .'

Neil drove me the short distance to Stratton Hospital. Hoping the balance of my mind was unimpaired I made my way through the quiet hospital to the waiting room and sat down next to a giant panda. Neil asked the panda if he had been waiting long. A nurse arrived and said there would be a few minutes wait. She may have wondered if my lump and the man who talked to large stuffed toys had any connection. My attempt to phone home was thwarted for I could not read the code. I wondered where my photo-chromic glasses were. They gave restful protection against the sea's reflected glare and I was wearing them when I arrived off Bude. The depressing answer came to me, as I knew the glasses were unlikely to, for they resided with my other lost items in the depths off Bude beach.

The nurse returned and ushered me in to see the doctor. He seemed happy with my lump. I believed the heavy copper-bound rudder, that had not been secured, had struck me as the breaking wave descended. The doctor believed, seeing the evidence, that my diagnosis was possibly correct. Sometimes I think I should have been a doctor. We took our leave, saying goodbye to the patient panda, and returned to Mevagissey.

TRAILER

Had I taken my unorthodox arrival at Bude as a sign, my story would have ended there, on a suitably dramatic note. Devon was only eight miles away and there was no sensible landing place before Clovelly on the north Devon coast. Sensibility had not interfered up to that point so I decided to try to take Epic right round Cornwall.

The day after my submarine arrival, Wednesday 13th, I returned to Bude to collect Epic. My younger brother Michael who was holidaying in Cornwall accompanied me. A couple of lengths of 2″x1″ timber had been left behind, so the oars (6′6″) were attached to the Fiesta's roof-rack to support Epic on the journey back home. Repair and modifications would take place back in Mevagissey.

After leaving the lifeboat hut I drove alongside the canal out of Bude, then headed north to check out Welcombe Mouth — a less than sensible landing place, eight miles away, just over the county border. We approached the beach by driving down narrow lanes and finally along a half mile rough track. Progress was very slow due to the projecting oars. I parked close to the cliff edge and walked over to view a comprehensive range of pointy rocks.

Over aeons the tops of folding strata had been eroded, leaving a series of toothed slabs running out into the ocean. The tide was out, having uncovered a few narrow sand strips between the close ranks of rock. A landing would have been possible in quiet conditions at low tide, such as we encountered, but it could well be a wet affair. It would also have been a drag to manhandle Epic to the black pebbles which formed a steepish slope at the high-water line, close to the cliffs. Remembering the Bude experience, I reckoned a high-tide landing would have advantages. Epic would sail over the natural breakwater formations and arrive close to the steep cliff-path.

Perhaps the idea of a circumnavigation came because I did not want the adventure to end. It would also be a tidy way of 'finishing off Cornwall' — taking Epic right round the County border. Cornwall is not an island, and I must admit that at first a circumnavigation seems rather an odd proposition. After looking at a map the idea does not seem so crazy — at least to me it did not. The Tamar, save for four miles, severs the counties. In reality, the northern extremity of the river is barely a trickle in the summer. That was of no consequence, for the border did not follow the course of the river exactly. After taking Epic overland I would re-launch some miles down-stream. Above North Tamerton there is a five square mile portion of Cornwall that lies east of the river. Below, the river divides the counties all the way down to the tidal waters below Gunnislake. Surely from North Tamerton such a modest vessel as mine would be able to drift down the mighty Tamar, I mused. To check would have taken away the mystery.

From the beach at Welcombe Mouth I hoped it would be possible to haul the dinghy up the cliff path. Help would not be sought, for up to then my trip round Cornwall had been unaided. Although assistance had been given in launching and loading, I could trace an unbroken track of solo progress with Epic, from Gunnislake to our separation in the surf off Bude.

The road section I reckoned was about twenty-five miles. The distance did not deter me, even though the first mile would include a rise of four hundred and thirty feet. I would build a set of wheels and, given time, push or pull Epic to North Tamerton, then drift down to salt-water; I mused on. To make life easier I would leave behind the mast, centreboard and rudder for the final coastal leg which would be rowed. The wooden mast, designed to be rigged with a gaff is very weighty, and the rudder, as my multicoloured forehead testified, was deceptively heavy.

After an intermission of a week or so there would be spring tides which would cast me high up the beach at a sensible time of day.

Thursday 14th. On the front lawn I glued back the wooden rowlock housing. The broken piece, luckily, still dangled on fibres of wood and it was a simple task to relocate, glue and screw it. Epic was ready for battle.

[You may not find trailer construction riveting. Feel free to skip a few paragraphs.]

Down in the studio, where I often produce watercolours of the cluttered shelves, I sorted out materials to create my transporter. The wheels came from an old bike that Edward had out-grown. (Wheels with an axle would have made construction much easier.) A simple framework was constructed from rough 2″x1″ timber left over after building a display for the 'Epic Voyage' exhibition. One length, a little longer than the boat's four feet eight inch beam, was laid on the floor. On to that, 6″ in from the ends, I glued and screwed two pairs of 10½″ uprights to hold the twenty inch wheels. Holes were drilled down into the centres of the timber uprights to take little devices taken from the rear wheel axle. (These consisted of washers, welded to a threaded shaft and used for tensioning the chain. They looked like miniature long handled ping-pong bats with holes in the flat part. I trust this is not too technical.) The fit was tight — just right to self-tap the bolt-ends. With the little 'bats' screwed home and aligned, I inserted the cogged rear wheel and nutted tightly. The outer uprights were strengthened with small shelf brackets.

At the counter of the upstairs cycle shop in St Austell Market House I asked for a pair of little bats and reflective red and white stickers. The use of rear wheel bats for a front wheel I easily explained, but the reason for doubling up on the stickers — because I was unsure from which end the inverted boat would be pushed, I found more difficult. From the ironmongers at the other end of the Market House I purchased half a dozen 'small shelf' brackets.

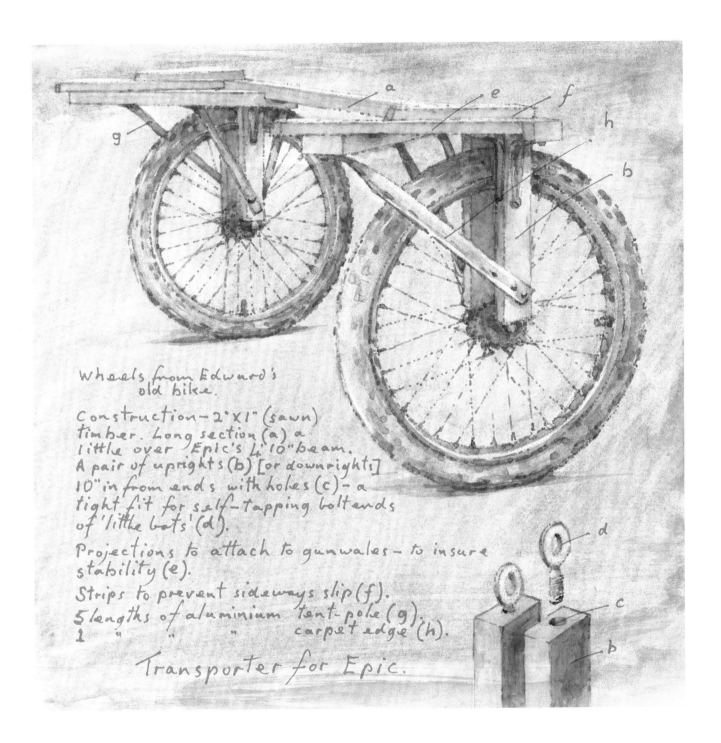

Wheels from Edward's
        old bike.

Construction - 2"x1" (sawn)
timber. Long section (a) a
little over 'Epic's 4' 10" beam.
A pair of uprights (b) [or downrights]
10" in from ends with holes (c) - a
tight fit for self-tapping bolt ends
of 'little bats' (d).
Projections to attach to gunwales - to insure
stability (e).
Strips to prevent sideways slip (f).
5 lengths of aluminium tent-pole (g).
1   "   "   "   carpet edge (h).
        Transporter for Epic.

With the wheels in place my construction looked plausible but still needed pieces of wood at right-angles in line with the gunwales, to stop the undercarriage folding. The extensions needed to project to one side only to ensure stability. The length of the extensions were just over a cubit (14″) or half that of a small shelf. (From feet and inch law you may think it regressive to return to Noah-measure. No, a cubit can be exactly one third of a metre — the length of a fore-arm. A metre has the disadvantage of not being divisible by three, metrically speaking. A 'dozenimal' system — one to eleven, then add a nought would be a good idea — even better than shelf measurement.)

For some time I deliberated, trying to work out a simple, lightweight method to attach the dinghy to the transporter. The solution involved two ten inch lengths of thin, red nylon guy-rope (scavenged from the remains of the old blue tent) passing through tiny holes drilled just below the gunwale (above if the boat is inverted). The red lines passing round the gunwales and the outer shelf-extension ends would hold the dinghy and wheel assembly firmly together. Small strips of timber were fitted on the half-shelves to prevent the boat from slipping sideways.

With the front end of Epic propped on a five foot length of 2″ x 1″ I secured the undercarriage to the inverted boat. On removing the prop I found Epic balanced beautifully. The hand positions, whether pushing or pulling from bow or stern, seemed a perfectly comfortable, mid-thigh height. Test run one began well. I progressed possibly six yards to the one inch rise leading from the front garden gravel to the road. The slight obstacle was too much — the structure creaked alarmingly and one wheel, quite independantly, turned inwards and the mission was aborted. The fourth and final test, six days later, was a robust success. Five pieces of aluminium tent pole — with ends beaten flat and drilled for screws, a flat length of aluminium carpet edge strip, two short lengths of 2′ x 1″ timber and a batch of 'small shelf' brackets were added by degrees as weaknesses emerged. It was a pity the sixth section of tent pole was missing — I lost style marks.

Captain's log June 20th. Two hundred yards past our house the lane is joined by a hill with precipitous gradients. It is so steep that a lower section has been grooved to facilitate tyre purchase. I heaved Epic thirty or forty yards up the hill and turned round in Ken and Sylvia's drive. It was a small step in relation to the portage envisaged but a pretty large leap for me. It was twenty five years to the day since the first men walked on the moon. Ken had met Buzz Aldrin. It's a small world — the moon.

I had decided to take the wheels with me from Bude and worked out a simple system to accommodate them. The same fixing points were used but the whole assembly was pivoted round so the wheels would be much further back, and not interfere with my rowing.

Three days later my new-look voyager would be transported to Bude. From there I would set out to complete the final leg — to Devon and another beach landing.

WHALE'S EYE and TALKING BOAT
(Bude to Welcombe Mouth and on to Darracott)

From the roof-rack of the Fiesta, which was parked at the bottom of the slip by the lock gates, Neil and I carried Epic fifty yards or so down the beach and set her beside the channel — to await the incoming tide. It had been eleven days since I had shepherded my wounded dinghy slowly up that same channel.

Our arrival at Bude, around 3:00pm, allowed plenty of time to load Epic with the reduced amount of gear and tie on the wheel assembly. Along with the weighty items I also left behind the red picnic box. Though a little cumbersome it was not all that heavy. It may have been black-listed for aesthetic reasons, or more likely in spite — for its poor showing at Bude.

I had no idea that such an interesting picture would develop as I prepared to photograph the be-wheeled Epic on the beach. To include the flooding channel in the shot I walked round the subject and was intrigued to see a red amphibious car driving out of the sea. I snapped the unusual convertibles together, then again as the boat-car drove by showing off twin propellers.

Minnie was on duty, so I walked down the beach to thank him for his help at the time of my previous arrival. There were many more people enjoying the seashore in the sunshine than on my first arrival. It was all very relaxing. For me, Bude had been rich in tide-line incident. I hoped the marine-car sighting (it was not another Minnie) would be the last unusual event to record before Bude was behind me.

The ocean flooded into the narrow channel. I pushed Epic into the deepening stream and rowed quickly out, over rounded seas, till the threat of breakers was passed. The Atlantic seemed in gentle mood — dark blue and dappled with wavelets. The cobalt heavens were brushed with misty white, and a little surf rolled onto the headland just north of Bude.

It was my last sea leg. Relief and sadness juggled with my emotions. My wish to finish with the demanding ocean also meant an end to the masochistic excitement. Happiness reigned — I was fit, in no apparent danger and knew exactly the location for the final beaching. In the meantime I had a most exquisite coastline of sun-warmed cliffs to enjoy as I glided by. Some of the vast faces were beautifully decorated with flowing seams of layered, contorted strata. Abrupt changes in the angles marked past geological conflicts resulting in fascinating, folded compositions.

The onboard fixing of the chunky BMX wheels and my wooden chassis worked well. The position did not hinder my rowing and I soon got used to the odd assemblage dominating the view. When four miles out from Bude, off Lower Sharpnose Point, I noticed a cluster of delicate-looking dish-aerials peeping over the cliff-top. They were a lot smaller than their more famous 'Goonhilly cousins' that I had sailed by at the other end of the county.

The trip had enabled me to explore and enjoy the varied coastline. Though I had no intention of circumnavigation at the onset, it now seems such a tidy goal — to end up where I started from. Such a simple concept — wait for fair weather and tides, then push off leaving the land to the right.

I rowed economically, for I planned my Welcombe arrival to coincide with high-tide at 7:00. There was a little less than three hours to cover a tide-assisted seven and a half miles. Those last idyllic hours were without urgency. I idled north wondering what lay in store at Welcombe Mouth. One imagined scenario saw Epic crash-landing, sustaining just enough structural damage to give me an even better excuse to stop than I had at Bude. Deep down though, I wanted to continue and hoped for a trouble free landing and possible cliff haul. It would have been a shame to waste those wonderful wheels.

Less than a couple of miles beyond Lower Sharpnose Point is Higher Sharpnose Point. Though projecting just a few hundred yards into the ocean it was a major landmark — the last headland before Devon. Appearing very tiny, beyond the great cliff, was the tower of a church. From my map I worked out that it belonged to the village of Morwenstow. The distant square of stone and the 'giant mushrooms' were the only visible signs of mans' occupation. It was so peaceful. The map also informed that just two miles on stood the gateway to Devon — which happened to be another Gull Rock.

Though not much more than a hundred yards in length that Gull Rock was mightily impressive. The evening sunshine filtering through the semi-mist showed off the powerful formation of the islet to good effect. From the side, the long awaited sea-mark resembled a great whale. It angled gently from the water, rising to form a rounded head crowned with draped strata — the vertical sides having succumbed to sea-power. The front of the whale's head pointed landwards and resembled the top half of a giant swiss-roll. The two dozen concentric, fossilised layers were being patiently digested by time. Surf tickled the tail sending white rivulets down the flanks.

Being ahead of schedule I had plenty of time to study in detail the structure of the whale-like Gull Rock. At high tide there is a thirty foot wide passage behind the Rock. While riding cautiously over the swells towards the gap I was excited to pass close by a tall, rectangular tunnel. It was where the eye of a whale should be. I could see through the seemingly precisely engineered gateway to the bright oblong of seascape the other side. The swells rose and fell, being sucked in and expelled as if the whale lived. I edged towards the opening. 'Please don't' I pleaded with myself as I felt the mischievous force. My copybook would not benefit from a further blotting. The temptation was so great. I really, nearly entered the whale's eye. Had there been width to work the oars satisfactorily I may have attempted to thread my way to Devon.

WHALE ROCK (Gull Rock)

'At high tide there is a thirty foot wide passage behind the Rock.'

The regimented structure of the whale shared the same remote, powerful magic as Fingal's Cave. Though I have never been to the location, I remember well the dramatic photograph on the sleeve of Grieg's popular Hebridean piece. With greater clarity I recall the overture music, crucial to a performing quartet of tutu'd ballet dancers, choreographed to synchronised perfection. The sequence was included in an 'Ace of Clubs' production, and I was one of those youth club dancers. We played it straight, and such was the success that we were asked to perform at other venues. Our allure, enhanced by tennis balls, was nullified when we leaped into view wearing outsize, studded boots. I never did think of becoming a dancer.

The channel round the back of the whale seemed non too wide as I rocked into Devon waters. I felt pretty chuffed — I had actually taken little Epic round the entire coast of Cornwall. The inner satisfaction was great but it was not the time or place to go completely overboard — I still had my final landing to accomplish. The constricted, swirling water gave way to calm and I headed across the bay towards Welcombe Mouth at the far end of the beach. Draining into the south side was Marsland Water — the county border. The twenty or so figures, close to the spot where I intended to land, were actually in Devon.

My imagined private landing was not to be. A few minutes later, on hearing the sound of a wave as it folded and crashed against a steep slope of rumbling pebbles, I thought it well to be a little public. At 6:45 I pulled hard for the beach hoping to ride in on one of the waves that rapidly formed within yards of the shore before extinguishing itself in the pebbles. Wearing shorts and flip-flops, I hoped to hop nimbly out of Epic and execute a hurried but casual haul up the few feet to dry pebbles. My run in was decisive. About five yards out I shipped oars and leaped ahead of a folding wave. Then, to my dissatisfaction, I sank to mid-calf in pebbles. Resembling an expanse of large shiny mussels, the flat stones, some up to six inches across, had been rendered relatively weightless after their engulfing. Before I could extricate myself, the following wave lifted the dinghy's stern, slewing the buoyant beast round for the gunwale to strike me aggressively on the thigh. In a moment of panic I managed to avoid being run over and was hastened up the slope by the frisky Epic. The onlookers, I hoped, would have thought it standard procedure. I tried to appear nonchalant.

For a moment, with elation boiling within, I stood somewhat traumatised. The cause was not the dead-legged landing but the fact that I was standing on a Devon beach. The sea voyage was over. Epic was whole and my hope for wheeled continuation was go.

Remembering the need for the Coast Guard to be informed of my safe arrival I asked a couple who were leaving the beach if they would make a call on my behalf. I would have liked to make the last phone-call personally, to sign myself off, but there were no public boxes anywhere near that remote spot.

A wave slapped the back of Epic and a little salty water doused the socks and jeans that I had foolishly left unprotected on the fore-deck. Not wishing the Atlantic a final, final fling, I dragged the dinghy a further few feet up the beach. I unloaded the boat and lay out my wet items on a large rock which faced a weakening sun. The removal of the wheel assembly — by releasing the little red bows was swift and simple. Epic rested on the beach, close to the cliff, at the bottom of a very steep slope. Up that daunting incline, not only Epic, but the wheel assembly, the oars and other clutter would have to be manhandled. There was no need for haste. I relaxed for a while. Soon enough I would have the beach to myself.

The sun gradually sank towards the misty-blue horizon, dancing its scintillating golden path over the ocean to the beach. Relaxing in the peaceful, pearly pink stillness, I enjoyed the calm. Matters seemed less urgent. I took my time, in tune with the surf's slow, rhythmic pulse. Unhurried groups left the beach, climbing the steep cliff path. In a little over an hour I was alone. It was time to tackle the climb. Epic looked larger and much heavier.

The most difficult part of the task was to raise Epic onto a narrow ledge about four feet up from the beach. On a forty five degree ramp formed with the oars I pushed the dinghy upwards. Because the lower part of the path was very narrow Epic had to be manhandled onto its side. A dinghy balanced on its gunwale is most unwieldy, I found coaxing the unruly boat the few yards to where the path widened and where Epic could be lowered right way up, an interesting though precarious challenge.

Two yards covered, twenty five miles to go. Had I bitten off too much? I had forgotten to bring my made to measure, five foot, boat prop. As well as an aid for fitting the wheel assembly it was to be a lever for boat manipulation. The oars became invaluable for levering, and more importantly, as slides on which to push the boat. I placed an oar at right angles under the lifted bow, heaved a little then lay down the second oar. Measured in half boat-length increments, Epic inched upwards. When the weight came off the rear oar it was squeezed back under the bow, marking another half boat-length claimed. More heaving, a couple of yards gained, and the process repeated, and repeated. After a while I would move the wheels and other gear up to the area of operation. The brass protective strip that ran under the boat was reduced in length by degrees as it broke up on rough outcrops. Looking on the bright-side I welcomed the reduction in weight. From the beach to the top of the slope where I would attach the wheels was about sixty yards (I imagined it to be at least a quarter of a mile, till I went back to check). As I inched upwards I perfected the procedure and was happy with progress. Once I realised I could reach the top, the task became quite therapeutic.

A couple of lady bathers on their way down to the beach for a late evening swim, asked, as they inched past what must have looked like the aftermath of an unusual shipwreck, if I needed help. I assumed they meant physical rather than counselling. My explanation of the single-handed nature of the circumnavigation may have confused the issue further.

Darkness was in the offing as I reached the dusty gravel at the top of the rise. In tired but triumphal haste I raised Epic's bow on crossed oars. Aligning the wheel carriage to the gunwales was akin to testing the triggering mechanism of a mantrap whilst being inside. Equilibrium was a swaying uncertainty till the red bows were tied. A pity my tailor-made jack-prop was still in Mevagissey.

It would have been possible to stow all the gear inside the inverted boat but I did not wish to test the strength of the trailer with the extra weight. My faith in the four little bats was still reserved. The oars were the heaviest and most awkward items. I intended to leave them behind as soon as a safe home could be found. For use on the river I had brought a pair of paddles — a legacy from the defunct rubber dinghy. They were in two sections — the bright yellow blades and blue handles were sealed, buoyant units — useful safety equipment and better than a life-ring for rowing down the river.

Most of my equipment fitted in a tatty, off-white sail-bag. My accommodation would be the sleeping-bag and a piece of heavy duty semi-transparent polythene about six feet square. My minimal tool-kit comprised a few brass screws, tacks, a roll of two inch, black fabric-reinforced adhesive tape and my trusty Swiss Army knife. A few sandwiches remained, and together with two Crunchy Bars, a packet of glucose tablets and three, half litre, plastic bottles of water (I set out with four), that was my fuel reserve. I carried a lightweight change of clothes and flip-flops, a small towel, soap, toothpaste and brush. Salt-water had deprived me of Walkman escapism. I did not replace the radio for I no longer needed the shipping forecast, and in any case I was unfolding my own personal mystery.

Having left the kit-bag and oars at the side of the rough track I headed eastwards into the dusk with my painting-bag over my shoulder. Even over the pot-holey surface the dinghy pushing was quite easy, though I worried about the durability of my construction. After a hundred yards or so I left Epic parked as off-track as possible, collected the sail-bag and oars and carried them on past the boat. With parking, pushing and porterage, my progress was about a quarter as fast (three times as far) as would have been a single loaded push. Within half an hour I passed from track to leafy lane, avoiding with sub-inch accuracy, contact with two carefully driven vehicles. Loaded with persons and branches the mini-convoy was, very likely, on barbecue business.

The OS informed of a PH (pub) one and a half miles inland at Darracott. An hour or so into the trek, at a lane junction, I came upon a heavenly sign. A slim oblong of white painted hardboard, nailed to a fence and roughly lettered in felt-tip, informed 'OLD SMITHY INN ½ MILE →'. My rate of progress was not enough to lift me immediately onto cloud nine. The half-mile (one and a half for me), the late hour and the double chevron symbol on the map — indicating an imminent steep hill, accelerated my mind into cunning plan mode.

SUNSET AT WELCOMBE MOUTH

'Darkness was in the offing . . .'

I left Epic on rough grassy ground by the dark, tree-canopied lane-side and headed speedily uphill. With oars and a plastic bag containing rowlocks, flares and life jacket, I arrived in good time to purchase a pint and beg storage for the unnecessary inventory. I spoke to Chris, a helpful young barman who directed me round the back to a stable where I could leave my stuff — there being no room at the Inn for suchlike.

Later, back down the lane, I crawled under Epic. After clearing away a quantity of the larger stones I spread out my plastic sheet. The luxury of sleeping under plywood was diminished by the sticks and remaining stones that interspersed the lumpy, cloddy soil. For the first time I had left behind my 'swiss-roll' — the roll of non-absorbent foam sheet often seen tied to the top, or hanging from the bottom, of back-packers' backpacks. The practically weightless item should not have been eliminated.

The sound of footsteps and the jolly banter of young folk, turfed from the Old Smithy, reached me as my head nestled into the sail-bag. If a boat appeared on your lane-side where one had not been when you walked along a few hours earlier, you might be inclined to tap it. Fresh from the pub, the lively youngsters made contact. After a few taps I thought it advisable to advertise my occupation. "Good-night" seemed a reasonable gambit, enough I hoped to dissuade a possible high-spirited relocation of my quarters.

"Hey! this boat talks." Further lighthearted boat communication broke out, then faded as all but one of the group weaved merrily on. The ensuing conversation was quite rational despite the improbable situation. Who felt most ridiculous I do not know. The voice from without enquired about my quest, and I from the darkness replied in a serious manner. Perhaps I was being humoured.

A GOOD MORNING'S WORK
(Darracott to North Tamerton)

At 3:50 I emerged from my lair into black night, extra darkened by tree cover. It was not the hard ground that caused my early rising, but excitement. You will think me easily pleased if setting out, pre-dawn, to test the feasibility of an arduous boat-walk excited me. I ate the chilly remains of my cheese and chutney sandwiches, then broached the second water-bottle, drinking a little and cleaning my teeth with a precious drop. The plastic sheet was soon folded and packed into a cubbyhole along with the water. Into the other I placed a polythene bag holding my foodstuffs. The sail-bag and painting-bag I wedged under the thwart. The tidy ship was ready for pushing.

Gripping my finely balanced charge by the stern I set off. The first test was immediate. There was no way up to higher ground without negotiating a steep hill with at least one chevron. I chose a route where in a two hundred yard climb I would cross one hundred foot's worth of contours. Ten steps, then rest against the boat. Ten more . . . rest . . . repeat. The gloom in the tunnel of trees reduced my world to a small area of toil. Earned pleasure is most rewarding. I knew that once at the top it would be all downhill — metaphorically speaking. Six inch steps — two hundred yards — six steps equals one yard — two foot-steps equal one foot — one foot after another, and another. By the time I bet myself I would reach the top with just six more stops the battle was nearly won.

I do not know how long it took to emerge from the tree-enclosed climb and reach the aptly sounding Welcombe village. Two hours after rising I crossed the main (A39) road — two and a half miles into the journey. Daylight had arrived by 5:00 along with a big round moon. I carried on down the deserted lane. The only sound from that still landscape came from the munching of unseen cows on the other side of the hedge. I rolled on, over the undulating Devon countryside.

Epic became a moving table. Once I had fished an item from inside the hull I did not return it — there was no one to tell me to tidy up. Food-bag, paint-bag, note-book and non-hyphenated items such as map, sponge, rope and an assortment of garments decorated the helpless craft. To facilitate my slovenly practise I tied a thin cord right over the boat to stop things falling off. Looking at photographs of 'Epic the overlander', often parked beside a sign-post, I am reminded of the similarly festooned carts belonging to goldfish-dispensing Steptoes.

The names of villages I passed through could have been a character list for a Dicken's novel. Let me introduce you to Ugworthy Barrows, Derrit and Pyworthy. All were left in my wake more swiftly and with greater ease than I could have possibly imagined when poring over the OS maps before setting out.

Sometimes pulling, I pushed on. On downhill sections, if not too downhill, I was inclined to jog. On one occasion, with my mind playfully engaged in estimations of journey completion times, I found myself carried away by the weighty momentum. Epic was then as near to destruction as at any time at sea. Wide-eyed and utilizing maximum reverse leg thrust, I avoided a five hundred feet above sea-level ship-wreck.

'8:21 Soldon Cross.' Then, *'9:45 cross main Bude / Holsworthy Rd.'* I was fifteen miles on from the beach landing and well into my encumbered road marathon — just ten miles to go.

Twelve years before I had thought, 'only eight miles to go'. I was running my first marathon. The previous year I had watched on television, participants in the first London Marathon. Towards the end they were crawling on hands and knees — they had hit 'the wall'. I had run a training fifteen miler two weeks earlier and was not wholly convinced about 'walls'. Something strange happened at the eighteen mile mark in the race — my legs stopped working. They were free agents and knew best. It was a physical impossibility to run an extra step. My sensible legs disengaged, then after a little staggering and a few minutes walking, permitted a light jogging session. Without the stagger, that pattern was repeated till merciful relief and a medal at Westminster Bridge.

I remember clearly that magical day when I tried to run my first marathon; also the rather less than magical night before. Arriving in London, late on pre-race day, I found a small hotel in which to relax. The accommodation turned out to be rather seedy. When I sat on the bed, the bottom near-side corner collapsed onto the threadbare carpet, dislodging a large empty coffee-tin and two Bibles. Retiring to the 'TV lounge' I entered a smoke-filled room, then withdrew immediately in order to preserve my lungs, un-smoked. They needed to be at their best for the next day's exertion. I sought the management and asked if an early breakfast could be available. 'Of course, and we'll get some Lucozade in', was not the response. My 'marathon participant status' plea, received something like 'No, breakfast's eight to nine.' After further pleading, I negotiated my taking a bowl of cornflakes to the bedroom and the promise of a pint of milk in the morning. The dining room was out of bounds — perhaps I was too great a risk, alone with the cruets.

With the support of the good books I slept well and an early milkman ensured an adequate breakfast. With an 'A to Z' in my hand I stepped onto the quiet Sunday streets and made my way to King's Cross. As I progressed, other persons — mostly single males wearing large, new white trainers, emerged and joined the flow. A trickle became a stream, then an orderly torrent escalated down to the Marathon specials that rattled loaded carriages of soon-to-be also-rans to Greenwich.

AFFALAND MOOR

'I followed the track across the rolling Affaland Moor.'

Camaraderie was extreme. It was an uplifting experience to participate. We soaked up inner saintliness, and vocal bonding was contagious, ". . . greased your nipples? I have Vaseline to spare". Personal bests' were secondary. Assisting fallers, sharing drinks and encouraging fellow sufferers was the order of the day. For most of us, alas, I fear our canonization was a temporary affair. It was agreeable to enter a world of fiction — of jogging Vikings and Mickey Mouses; and if only for a day, leave the rat-race.

We will leave the congested streets of London and return to a peaceful Devonshire lane. About five miles from my proposed river entry point, instead of turning left and keeping to the roadway, I carried on to within a few yards of the county border. The OS showed an 'other road, drive or track' that led to a lane that crossed the little River Deer. I was lucky to notice the dirt track on the other side of a metal gate, for there were no directions. Faded lettering on a rough plank tied to the gate, read ' . . EASE SHUT CAT .'. Entry to the field was hampered by a herd of inquisitive Friesians who came to greet the strange 'headless white'.

I followed the track across the rolling Affaland Moor. Interspersed with gorsey, scrubby areas were occasional groups of trees under which cows and sheep escaped the heat of the sun. Half a mile on I came upon a boggy patch. To round the obstruction meant a detour over uncertain terrain. Rocks and bricks had been tossed into the mire to lessen the depth. I slipped on my flip-flops and squelched the lurching Epic across the testing obstacle. The undercarriage came through with distinction; I with growing confidence and slimy feet. A circumnavigation seemed more than speculation.

I eased Epic down the track to the little bridge at Forda Mill. After crossing the river, which surely is a stream, there was a long push up to the road that in three miles would take me to North Tamerton. The nearness of my goal made that very steep climb between high banks, where I ascended two-hundred feet, a greater certainty and therefore more pleasurable than my pioneering ascent nine hours earlier.

'12:14pm North Tamerton 2 miles.' There was little traffic, and pedestrians were few. One bright spark could not resist telling me I was a long way off course. Without time to explain my purpose in pushing a boat at altitude, I cantered by. Horseflies were the reason for the rapid rate of knots at the time. I was deep in cow country and they were finding the scent of my exertions irresistible.

At 1:00pm exactly, I stopped on a small, single arched bridge that spanned a pool of dark River Deer that lurked between steep banks. Trees overhung the ever-so-slowly-flowing tributary (which met the main river just two hundred yards downstream). Down the road, two minutes away, was the River Tamar. It had all happened so quickly. Far from being the most difficult part of the endeavour, the wheeled trek had been the easiest. A good morning's work. I rested Epic's stern on the tarmac and sat on the parapet.

Studying the map, I made a discovery — the field bounded by the lane and the two rivers was Cornish. Had I put Epic directly into the Tamar the circumnavigation would have been incomplete. I needed to round those few acres of grazing land. As I pondered my predicament I was joined on the bridge by an old boy and his dog. With reciprocal compliments expressed, regarding dog and boat, I asked the gentleman if he knew who owned that particular piece of Cornwall.

"Mr Hobbs won't mind you using his field."

Not dwelling on the legality of the generous invitation — to use a third party's land, I wheeled Epic down the road. Feeling rather guilty, I opened the gate and entered the field a few steps away from a graceful stone arched bridge that spanned the youthful Tamar. My first view of the upper reaches was quite sobering. Epic could have floated happily on the bridge-pool, but distressingly, the outward flow was no more than six feet wide and very, very shallow. It was to join the Deer a few yards downstream, and not too far away the Claw. Surely the combination of all that water would be sufficient to float me down to Morwellham. I trundled Epic the last few wheeled yards over deep grass, back up to the Deer bridge, and prepared to launch. The whole story was unfolding beautifully. In blissful ignorance I believed I was stepping from dairy-land to fairy-land. 'Hark, a merry tinkling, the popping of iridescent dewdrops showering stardust . . .'

ANGEL FISHERMAN
(North Tamerton to Boyton Bridge)

Without the slightest inkling that all was not to be plain sailing I depleted my sparse food and drink reserve — devouring two bananas and consuming an extravagant quantity of water. Refuelling would be made at waterside establishments, I assumed. What waterside establishments? you may be thinking. Between riverside shops and pubs I may have had it in mind to pluck grapes and the occasional peach from overhanging boughs as I drifted by.

Although still in a field, Epic looked happier the right way up. I fixed the wheels further back — as for the last sea leg, then tied loops of cord to the rowlock holes — for use with the little paddles. Between clumps of thistles and a few wands of foxgloves I launched Epic vertically down an eight foot bank, taking on board, over the stern, a quantity of non-drinkable water. I dropped my 'luggage' down onto the fore-deck and precariously followed, lowering myself from tussocks. Epic floated on brown water in the shade of overhanging trees while I sponged out the dinghy and positioned the ridiculous midget oars. I thought it was of no consequence that the proper oars were still stabled — for they were too long to fit between the banks. At a speed that would barely have seen off a tethered pudding, I thrashed my way a few yards up to the Deer bridge. Had I not, there would still have been a thin strip of Cornwall non-circumnavigated.

The loop/rowlock idea was a total failure, but it did not matter. With a paddle in each hand, butterfly-stroke fashion, I headed the few yards to the Tamar. I passed out of the shade and before reaching the 'mighty river', rounded a bend and met foliage and shallow water. Wearing my flip-flops I stepped into the cool unknown. My feet became intimate with mud and weed, and I sensed the presence of piranhas and electric eels. Back on board I drifted a few more yards. The sun warmed my sun-hat and glinted on flowing water ahead. Silent flitterings of electric-bluey-green damselflies entertained me. I recorded the joyous moment in my log-book. '. . . *peace beautiful. Quietly drift — cover legs — sun. V hot — nice breeze sometimes 2:36 just paddled — off — now drift perfection!'* and on that note I exited fairy-land.

There began a journey to tidal waters; a journey unlikely to be repeated, for there is just too little water. Not enough for a small canoe, or even a large washing-up bowl. It soon became apparent that I would be afloat very little in the early stages. Though rowing more than an odd stroke was off the agenda, till 'at least round the next bend', the wooden oars would have been very useful as rollers, sliders or levers. One of the first pools upon which I was able to float was a twenty-five to thirty foot wide, leafy canopied affair that provided cool shade. The retreat was occupied by paddling cows. The herd — palomino, russet and black and white coloured, were fairly still as I paddled towards them. They became a little inquisitive as I wove within hoof steps of two mid-brown ones. To prevent the cattle wandering, barriers of single or double strands of barbed-wire were stretched across the river in many places. The height of the pneumatic tyres was a problem — I was lucky not to be punctured.

PADDLING COWS

'They became a little inquisitive as I wove within hoof steps of two mid-brown ones.'

Between the odd pools where Epic could float I splashed alongside or walked on the exposed gravel bed whilst guiding the dinghy along narrow rushing channels, no wider than itself. Where the river was wider the hull grazed the stony river bed and needed coaxing over even smallish tones. The flimsy ply hull ruled out rushing. When not immediately downstream from wading cows the water was reasonably clear and flip-flops seemed ideal footwear, at first. Quick-drying shorts and a shirt completed my ensemble.

Before clocking up the first mile I encountered what looked like a beaver's lodge. The huge dam of branches and twigs had been caught in a riverside tree at the height of a winter's flood. The impenetrable barrier stood five feet high so a slight detour over the grassy bank was required. I was travelling light so there was no need to unload. Epic slid over the deep grass with comparative ease. Those first obstructions, I should have realized, would not be the last. Flowing in from the left the River Claw joined the Tamar, theoretically boosting the flow but making no apparent difference. By that time I had progressed half a mile south. That was 'crow-measurement', the twisting Tamar at least doubled that distance. The OS showed, below the Claw, many little streams adding to the volume of water which would surely build up the power to whisk Epic effortlessly down to Gunnislake.

Alone, I moved slowly through a tranquil landscape. Apart from glimpses of reflected sky and breaks in the tree canopy, a full, lush spectrum of greens pervaded. The river slipped quietly past spits of exposed gravelly riverbed, then on, gently scouring and chuckling to new, dark pools.

When two and a half hours or so into the trek — with a little over one crow-mile travelled, I sighted a fine, stone, shallow-arched bridge of similar proportions to the North Tamerton one. A chance to replenish supplies and find out where deeper water could be expected, I presumed. I dragged Epic's bow onto a shallow bank of small angular, pale, pinky-browny-purple stones, the same colour as the bridge, then sauntered up to the absolutely deserted, little trodden grass track that so gracefully spanned the river. On the plus side, it was extremely peaceful and picturesque; but I was in need of drinking water, and could have murdered a cream tea with extra scones.

Thwarted, I paddled off downstream with Epic in tow. Pools on which I could float for a few yards were still rare, often ending with an obstruction that resulted in portage. Every fifty to a hundred yards I undertook a haul down mini-rapids. Difficulties with shallow water and overland hauling necessitated the rapid under-standing of the art of driftwood manipulation. Placed crossways under the dinghy, soft slippery timbers allowed Epic to be dragged onwards using less energy. It was a pity that sections of the brass strip were lying on the cliff slop — the hull would have slid more easily had it been intact. Two or three pieces of wood, arm-length and thickness, were ideal for the task. One major obstruction demanded a thirty yard or so detour along a sloping and undulating sandy bank. A selection of contorted lengths of branch — readily available from the dam, were used to help prevent sideways slip. As a user of logs in boating I have few equals.

Early into the haul I was perturbed to find a leech fastened to my right calf. Being a non-smoker I resorted to finger-flicking the 'beast' away. If it was the blood-sucking variety that inflates to sausage size in seconds I was not prepared to research the matter.

Hours passed. Pretty tired and very thirsty I laboured on, expecting at every turn to see a bridge. From North Tamerton to Boyton Bridge (almost due south) the distance is just over three 'crow-miles'. Not knowing my speed I could not judge my arrival time at Boyton Bridge — my first objective.

The visual pleasure gained while negotiating the river was a precious experience. It is fortunate that the less pleasant times quickly fade. Several hours of the haul were expressed by a single word in the log-book — *'hell'*.

It had been six hours since my communication with the man who knew Mr Hobbs when I detected a movement between the trees. Some yards downstream a fisherman was working his way up towards me, casting his fly between the stones, seeking a trout in the deeper 'puddles'. Sometime before I shouted my apology for spoiling the fishing, the laid-back angler told me he ". . . could hear an occasional rumbling, then it would be quiet for a few minutes . . . sounded like some prehistoric monster." Bill Dinner then saw between the trees the white triangle of Epic's flat bow. He wandered up and, for one who had had his world desecrated, greeted me kindly. " . . . I was about to stop fishing anyway . . . have never seen anything like it in my life."

Bill, a Boyton man, was as surprised as I was relieved at our meeting. He told me boats had not been in the vicinity since the Bude canal had closed. Bill, whose great, great-grandfather had been a wharfinger at Boyton, brought good tidings — I would shortly reach a long pool that would lead to Boyton Bridge, just a few hundred yards away. Then better news — he would shortly be driving to The Countryman — a hostelry a mere three and a bit miles away where evening meals were available. He would give me a lift if I wished. Fortunately the car would travel a good deal quicker than the half mile per hour I had managed on the river, which was as well, for we had only forty five minutes to reach the pub before last food orders were called.

Half an hour later I had pulled Epic up onto a grassy bank in a field to the left and downstream from a mundane iron bridge. The flat structure, less picturesque than the usual stone, arched variety, was a most welcome sight for me at the time. The sandwiches consumed at North Tamerton were a distant memory. In no time I was being whisked 'foodwards'. Major refuelling was required and a large steak played the leading role in my gastronomic fantasy.

After freshening up (I took a towel and toothbrush to the pub) I pulled my Norwegian jumper over a rather grubby shirt and settled upon a bar-stool. Perched, pint in hand and with the knowledge that my medium rump, claimed at the nick of nine o'clock, was on the griddle, I was in paradise.

The barman Phil refilled my remaining three, half litre water-bottles. Still on cloud nine I was returned to Boyton Bridge. Perhaps Bill Dinner is an angel — a lone fisherman would be a plausible front. He was at least the instigator of a heavenly interlude. Extremely tired but free of cares, I climbed over the gate and returned to the dinghy. Epic lay in a hollow, out of sight behind a grassy hump. There I also lay — in the sleeping-bag, on the orange plastic bag. The grass was soft. I slept soundly.

BRIDGE BEFORE BOYTON

'. . . I sighted a fine, stone, shallow-arched bridge of similar proportions to the North Tamerton one.'

PUNCTURED PLYWOOD
(Boyton Bridge to Netherbridge)

Bats fluttered in the stillness. Fish rose — imagined rings in the darkness. Up at five, then back to bag. The river still and black. My private night-time space expanded. *'. . . can see the bridge birds singing — after crickets chirp. Soon be light enough to start. Dark under trees on river.'* The pool had no end — it would be miles at least, and I would soon be drifting and paddling southwards. I cleaned my teeth and drank half a bottle of water — leaving me with two and a half. My remaining rations — two crushed Crunchy bars and a packet of glucose tablets, were an incentive to reach another 'Countryman' without delay. The next pub would surely be closer to the river, for I could not expect to be saved again by another 'Dinner-man'.

At 5:50 I slipped Epic stern-first into the river. It took little time to decamp, load and leave without trace of occupation. Early on — perhaps still on the first pool, I encountered a downed tree obstruction. Lying across the river at water level was a large trunk. Positioned a little above it, as if on purpose, a hefty bough seemed to suggest a detour. It was ironic that a rare drift, on a lovely deep pool, should be halted because that particular tree happened to fall in a particular way. Before heading back upstream to find an exit point I ran Epic onto the lower, half submerged trunk. There was just a possibility that I could juggle the wheels below the upper branch which formed a shallow arch. Standing on the lower, with my arm over the upper part of the barrier, I heaved and squeezed Epic through. Fine dusty silt, that had been filtered from the river in spate, puthered into my hair and eyes. I could not stand back to photograph, but I can picture a Mirror dinghy held in 'tweezers' above a dark still pool. There is more than meets the eyes in circumnavigating.

Soon I was back to paddling, pushing and pulling. The lack of water was a major annoyance, except on one occasion when there was too much. *'Lost Epic . . .'* the note reminds me of the episode. My charge had not disappeared but was beyond reach for a while. Sticky red mud at the side of a deep pool prevented me reaching the pesky dinghy. Epic had been blown to the Cornish side where it bobbed back and forth against a six foot hight cliff. There were no long sticks to hand (to coax, not to thrash) so I made my way round to the field opposite. From there I dangled, till I caught the gunwale with my foot. The gymnastic physics engaged to board was tricky. Sideways motion and tipping were avoided with an undignified flop-cum-sprawl.

The still water attracted swarms of flies, so breakfast was taken a few hundred yards down-stream where I devoured one of the Crunchy bars. It was only 7:00am. Two hours later, Epic was parked beneath the green canopy on an expanse of exposed red rocky riverbed. Although boughs of peaches were seeming less likely, I still polished off the last Crunchy bar.

Investigating among the little shale slabs I chanced upon a small frog. That is how hungry I was (only joking). Not knowing frogs could be that small I photographed the specimen. Against the blue of OS 190 I snapped the froglet. The wind was getting up, which accounts for the weighty stone placed three nautical miles south of the tiny, out of focus, frog. The minute specimen was an unfortunate subject for wild-life photography, bearing in mind my rather basic camera has no other function than making everything look a long way off. Had I met an elephant there would not have been a problem (other than the smallness of my map). Even though the frog is just a blur I can calculate its overall length — which is a quarter of an inch, the size of the lettering in the map title. The photograph also reveals a smaller object, about a mile and a half south west of Hartland Quay. No small island exists in that area, so I rather think it was a bit of twig. A slight stain remains on the map, confirming the position where the frog posed. DNA may be present; so it is just possible that in the future, a character versed in the sciences and possessing an inquisitive interest in cartography, may trace the trace and have the tiny amphibian recreated. (Film rights reserved.) The mini-frog could be called Atlantis.

On a few hastily written lines in the logbook there is evidence of 'waterproof' ink running. *'Writing on Raindrops* (a good title) . . . *rain blowing up the valley   Quite wet 10.30 shelter under trees — watch rain driving in front of trees across fields opposite. I'm getting damp now. Ugh!! Wonder where I am. Feet sore.'* Even though what I was doing was odd I thought it was a good thing for me, and on the whole had enjoyed it immensely. A good thing though is what you can have too much of, and I was beginning to reach that stage.

The rain ceased and I had progressed a further, hard won, half mile, when a noise, hardly dramatic, came from the front end of Epic. As I knelt on the fore-deck, whilst easing the boat into a pool, there was a kind of splitting sound. I had foolishly attempted to be afloat — perhaps for the novelty value. The water was murky and lurking rocks were plentiful. A similar sound a few seconds later, I assumed, was further splitting of the flimsy deck. Later I realized a lurking rock had punctured the plywood. With so little water in the river it was not surprising that several minutes passed before the holed area was submerged long enough to flood the front cubbyholes and the problem be manifest. I sought a location clear of tree cover and light enough to inspect the damage. Lo, there was light at the end of the tunnel — beyond a straight stretch ahead. Double lo, there was also an arched bridge, barely discernible in the distance. I towed my wounded Epic on, wondering what services would be available at the crossing. A boat repair workshop would have been nice, but I would have settled for a shop and a chance to purchase a pie, or possibly a peach.

At noon I reached Druxton Bridge — a beautiful four-arched structure, larger than, but similar to the one carrying the grassy track that I encountered the previous day. A few yards from the bleached pink stone bridge, I lifted Epic's bow clear of the river onto a slight gradient that led towards the road. Expectantly, I sauntered to the metalled highway. A lonesome sign informed 'Launceston four miles'. It was an extremely quiet part of Devon. There was an equally quiet part of Cornwall over the bridge. For a while I enjoyed the rare silence — free from my splashings and the hollow tortured sounds from the dragged dinghy's hull. Had I ventured along the lanes — seeking a food shop, I feared my foraging would be fruitless. The peaches would have to wait.

Before continuing the rocky, watery grind, I had to patch poor Epic. A few large stones were needed to prop up the bow of the abused boat. I could have sworn I had been traversing a rocky landscape yet there was no suitable material on hand. Had Epic not just been punctured by a specimen, and had I not recently slithered over tons of the stuff. Perplexed, I wandered upstream to hunt for large rocks. Having located a few of the rare mineral specimens, I staggered back over the slippery riverbed. A piece of plywood — the size of a fifty pence piece had been pushed in. It was a clean wound, forward and above the multi-scarred lower section. I dried it with my shirt sleeve and paper tissue, then friction-warmed it — rapidly rubbing with grubby cuff. With Swiss Army knife and the roll of two-and-a-half-inch-wide, fabric-reinforced, black sticky-tape, I effected the repair. The patch still sticks, limpet-like, to this day.

My lunch, a glucose tablet and 'Countryman' water was followed by crumbs from the Crunchy bars, fastidiously reclaimed from the food bag. The tiny morsels punished my taste buds. A note in my log book suggested I take the red picnic box next time. Not only would be foodstuffs remain cool and intact but I should feel tempted to lay in a greater store.

'. . . leave 12:35. More barbed-wire — 4th lot?' There are people who collect short lengths of varying types of barbed-wire. I have never been fond of it, and even if there had been a latent spark before the trip, it would now be snuffed out. A little sketchy drawing of three strayed strands of the vicious spiky stuff adorn the log-book page from which I am now working. Passing under the wires would have been easier had I detached the wheel assembly.

Physically and mentally I was losing efficiency. I began to talk to the boat. As if the painter were a lead, I led and coaxed, "Come on Epic." Flip-flopped feet slipped on downstream. Pulling, pushing and leaning on my trusty Epic when in danger of falling, I continued. Shallows were a little less than continous; and deeps, anything over a foot, were short and of nuisance value only. Occasionally I would notice rows of blankly staring cows looking down from the banks — the diversion exciting them into a few moments of standing still.

DRUXTON BRIDGE

'A few yards from the bleached pink stone bridge, I lifted Epic's bow clear of the river onto a slight gradient that led towards the road.'

The verdant mono-colour world, wonderful though it was, would occasionally be treated to a shock of fleeting colour that would alert the senses.

> An exception to the rule of green
> a micro-second pleases,
> Kingfisher against white hull
> as different from chalk as cheese is.

Deep down I must have realised that the end was some way off, but funnily enough I never thought of calling it a day. As if programmed I was drawn to the next bend — a little bit closer to tidal waters. Every detail of Epic, from the chipped and rotten bow to the bent pintles on the stern, were so familiar. Each item of my motley gear had its place — and what a comic collection I carried. It was fortunate that human eyes did not see me at 'work'. The ludicrous blue and bright yellow paddles and the cycle wheels would have provided some amusement. Three very useful mini-logs had joined the permanent inventory. They rested on the back seat when not being used to coax Epic down-river. One fine specimen had a protuberance at one end — a most useful tool.

After making my way through the branches of yet another downed tree I picked my way slowly down a series of rapids. Ahead, I spied the slightly curved, reinforced concrete span of the A388 road-bridge (Nether Bridge). The water deepened, I boarded Epic and battled with the 'toy' paddles. A gusty wind wasted no time in rushing up that wide, straight expanse of exposed river. I minded not those few minutes of exertion, for the bridge was just two miles from Launceston — two miles from a wad of restaurants.

Fifty yards or so beyond the mighty span stood another fine, four-arched, stone bridge. The intimate scale of the old bridge afforded greater privacy than the open-plan of the new version; particularly under the near-side Devon arch which protected a small pool. Approaching from downstream, Epic just grazed into the haven. A few large stones prevented my drawing Epic tightly into the bank. While de-stoning the berth, a sneaky, fierce gust of wind sent Epic back upstream. My speed in pursuit was always slightly less than the dinghy's. It floated high and skitted mischievously out of reach. In two steps the river lapped my knees and in four it was mid thigh. Soon I struggled on with water up to my waist and flip-flops adrift. Such irony — I had battled for hours down a watercourse grandly designated a river and impersonating a ditch, and when reaching deep water suffered the ignominy of wading. I collected Epic, retrieved flip-flops and skulked back to my lair.

My farcical arrival, as far as I know, went unnoticed. If that is so, my time on the river had been witnessed solely by the great, great grand-son of a wharfinger. I was thankful for that mercy.

Clouds were growing and greying. There were still sunny periods so I hung my wet shorts on a twig. My damp legs I coaxed into jeans, and sore puffy feet into unyielding socks. It would have been about 3:30 and I was about to hit Launceston — to recharge, ready for the final push. In a couple of days, with much balmy floating, I 'should' have completed my circumnavigation.

Before heading into town I ensured my drying shorts were securely anchored, for the wind was increasing. The surface of the river was dashed with ranks of small sharp waves marching upstream, and a few heavy raindrops found their way through the trees. A little wind and rain would do no harm for it was July and I was no longer at the mercy of the sea. Perhaps I should have taken heed of the 'flapping shorts' portent.

A BRIDGE TOO FAR
(Near Launceston)

From under the bridge I took a picture — the last on my last roll. Trees, a field or two back across the river were losing definition in a descending, misty dampness. Epic, stripped bare, save for the wheel assembly, was being thoroughly cleansed.

Still optimistically cheerful, I placed most of my belongings against the upstream side of the bridge, out of sight and rain, and headed towards the region of plenty. Fortunately, showers were few and light, for my oilskin was still, I presumed, in the Atlantic ocean. Speculating that it might be the last night before journey's end I gaily set out for Launceston. I headed towards a picturesque castle perched on top of a steep hill. The simple form, which dominated the landscape, looked like a child's design, even without a huge flag flying. Had it not been for the tarmac, I could have imagined myself in a previous century, walking towards the historic town. I was not totally 'transported' — there being no hay-carts, knights on horseback or folk trussed up in sacking and thonging. I wended my way, kept on my toes by the spasmodic rushings of combustion engines.

At 5:30 I entered the town, purchased thirty six exposures, and set about relieving my ravenousness. Ale-house temptations were resisted quite easily — not only were my sleeping quarters two miles away, beside a river that possessed a malicious humour and varying depths; but it was early on a Monday evening and Launceston was not exactly buzzing. Soon I chanced upon 'The Launceston Fryers' and was tucking into fish'n'chips, mushy peas and faggots and gravy. Even in the most adventurous cuisine I doubt if fish and faggots share a plate. However, twelve hours of hard labour, fuelled solely by two Crunchy bars and a few glucose tablets, changes one's perspective. Presentation and convention were not uppermost in my mind.

A time of great misery was about to unfold; and that may be an understatement. I strolled contentedly away from Launceston, retracing my steps, heading down a steep hill away from the castle. The road direction seemed to be heading too north-westward for my liking so I decided to take a shortcut. It added over a mile to the return journey. A persistent drizzle started as I began my meandering, intensifying my wish to rejoin Epic at the soonest.

A condition that first manifested itself on the Boscastle to Bude leg became quite uncomfortable. It had been a spasmodic, irritating tingle in the region of my left shoulder-blade. I imagine it was caused by doing more pushing and pulling than usual. I had tried to be lenient with the muscles in the affected area, but even dangling my arms did not ease the discomfort. In an attempt to lessen the strain I walked with my hands on my head, then with arms folded, then with alternate hands on opposite shoulders, but relief was short lived.

LAUNCESTON CASTLE

'I headed towards a picturesque castle perched on top of a steep hill.'

I wanted to be back under the bridge — lying down, wrapped in my polythene sheet. To make my wish come true (I am easily pleased) I decided to phone for a taxi. Phone boxes were a taxi-ride away and as there were no taxis, I trudged gloomily on through the gloom. A large car stopped beside me before exiting a driveway. A stroke of luck, I must have thought. Standing in the rain, I grovellingly explained my situation and need to make a phone-call. If I carried on I might possibly come across a phone-box, I was informed. The man may have been car-proud and not wished to let in a damp biped. Not all was lost, the car was followed by another. I benignly bent to the second car which did not stop. The 'pharisees' drove away. All was lost. Half an hour later, after a right-hander and two left-handers, I was back in Launceston.

A wearysome while later I arrived at my bridge and took stock of the situation. The drizzle had turned to rain and drove in under the bridge at an increased angle. My mini-logs, which prevented me getting bogged down when unloading, were squashed into the mire beside the floating dinghy. I contemplated how best to utilise my equipment. Though I did not expect to be entirely bushy-tailed the following morning, I hoped still to be operational. The rain became heavy and horizontal. Trees thrashed wildly and darkness was falling. I retreated with my bivouac items to a mossy ledge at the downstream side of the arch, a few yards from where Epic strained against the tether. I use the term bivouac loosely. The sloping ledge was two and a half feet wide and a foot or two above ground level. Daylight fizzled out along with my options.

There are times when looking on the bright-side calls for a degree of imagination. Only a vestige of dimness remained, and the 'end in sight' feeling had also faded. Strangely enough, I occupied the windward ledge. The nearness of large trees and a peculiar wind tunnel effect caused the seemingly more sheltered ledge to receive a severe lashing, while my perch was reasonably dry, at first. One of my major 'bivouacal' items — the square of heavy-duty polythene, was in a cubbyhole on the dinghy. Darkness, driving rain and squidgy mud ensured it remained there. I unzipped the sleeping-bag to form a square then folded it about my person, holding two corners and trapping the others under my 'trainered' feet. My footwear encouraged the wind to circulate, sucking in the rain and efficiently dispersing, in a few minutes, all the warmth from my feet. The open end of the plastic survival bag I held against the vertical stonework with my head, and the other end I clutched along with the sleeping bag, saving my upper body from the odd large drip and intermittent, wayward drifts of rain. Thus it was that my awful night began.

The pressure required to trap the orange bag soon caused my neck and shoulders to ache. To alleviate the problem the plastic bag had to be coaxed behind my back — not that easily achieved in a wind-tunnel. There was less plastic protection and my grip had to be higher. Clawing together the blue and orange bags caused my fingers to weaken and the sleeping-bag kept escaping, causing unwanted cooling. Resting my elbows on my knees brought some relief but I had to continually readjust my position. The wind increased, probing more searchingly and funnelling more rain my way.

Gravity would have its way and I continually had to counteract the slippery slope. Squashed moss lacks traction. I would move a foot, when edging myself back and set my bag a-flapping. The lower part of the sleeping bag began to get wet, then wetter. Gradually the waterlogging crept up to my knees. My jeans then acted as secondary wicks to ensure thorough numbing. Eventually I managed to draw the sleeping bag over my head and hold it in place with the orange survival bag. In the quieter dark I contorted and squirmed into position to operate my watch. Time itself had slowed. Checking after an hour would indicate a five minutes advancement. My Casio boasted an illumination function, but no fast forward button.

The night was so long and I was so cold and achy.* The misery built up, and finally I could take no more. That vestige of spark was finally extinguished. At that time of deepest despair I made the decision to give up. I decided I would ask for police help. The thought of a dry prison cell in Launceston, relived the mental torture briefly. The pain 'was' soon to stop. Reality dawned. Although I was within a hundred yards or so of a main road, there was no easy escape. (To proper 'bivouac people' this must seem a pathetic whinge.) After a clamber up the muddy bank in a howling rainstorm in the pitch dark, I would make my way to the, infrequently used at night, roadway, and . . . What would I be wearing? — my square of heavy-duty polythene, a soaking sleeping bag weighing at least a hundredweight, or perhaps an orange survival bag with a hole cut for my head and two for arms for signalling purposes. I would wait for headlights to appear, flag down the vehicle and ask to be taken to the nearest police station. Hmmm. If the first few motorists drove on by I must not be dispirited. Would you stop for a large piece of litter or something resembling a giant sausage?

During the course of the night the wind and rain moderated. I sensed the change from inside my miserable cocoon. Many times I peeped out, but for no reward — it was so dark, difficult to know if my eyes were even working. Dawn was late in coming — it seemed like lunch-time. I had been a pupa too long. Squatting on that once mossy ledge I was shocked from darkness when a routine lifting of the damp bag was met with blinding light. It was 6:00am and I almost fell of my perch. The extending boundaries revealed a world that promised no immediate pleasure. I unfurled my numbed body and stood in the mud, under the bridge, and wished I was at home.

One phone-call would end the ordeal for me, but Epic had to be sorted out. If the dinghy could remain tucked away under trees, close to the bridge, I would be a free agent. I would walk up the hill to a handy Devonshire farm a quarter of a mile away, and see if Epic could be left for a few days. 7:00 would be the earliest I dared ask for the favour.

* *'Beep beep'. The word processor did not think much of 'achy'. (There it goes again.) At times it takes charge. Correcting a misspelt sausage, I overlooked a bleep-less 'assuage'. It is all very well, but I can not be 'sausaged'. 'Beep beep'.*

While coldly kicking my heels I decided not to call it a day as far as the voyage was concerned. I hoped my return would see me in deep water — in the nicest possible way, and I would be able to do a bit of serious floating.

I was not to know that the farmer did not live at the farmhouse. Though I had been patient, it was still a very early hour for a regular household to receive a visitor. After ringing the bell, it seemed an awfully long time before I detected sound then saw a light go on. I wished I was still under the bridge. There was no reprimand. After a hurried apologetic explanation for my behaviour I was granted my wish — by proxy again, as the farmer lived next door. The kind treatment from the Devon gentleman buoyed me up considerably.

Before setting off to the farm I had studied OS 201 in some detail — there being few recreational activities available to me. The map shows a phone symbol at the village of Liftondown — two hilly miles away from 'my' bridge. It was in the opposite direction, but the same distance away as Launceston. Having previously walked from the old county town I opted for change and decided to phone home from Liftondown. The weather remained miserable — I encountered drizzle interspersed with heavy showers. My jumper was synthetic and did not completely protect me from the downpours. Sheep are lucky — both in sporting wool and not wearing denim. My jeans became even more water-logged, and very heavy.

After such a torrid night my early morning walk was relatively soothing. The warmth generated was a major factor. Not wishing to disturb my family at too early an hour I made my excursion into Devonshire a leisurely affair. In the shelter of a roadside tree, during a sharp deluge, I pondered my unusual situation. There were few downs really, and the present one would soon be history. The ups outweighed overwhelmingly. Simple everyday pleasures lurked, or may have lurked round each corner. A pint, a long pool, dry feet and even mushy peas pleased.

Before 9:00 I was back under the bridge preparing for my strategic withdrawal. My phone-call caused no inconvenience — in fact Robin seemed almost eager to drive over and collect me. It was quite uplifting to know that when the need arises, willing help is there. The family unit is a wondrous thing. The location of my plight just happened to be en route to an extremely heavy amplifier that required urgent collection from the wilds of Devon. The rocking chauffeur would arrive at 10:00ish on his way to collect the coveted piece of equipment.

Meanwhile I unpacked, bailed and sponged out Epic. I then removed the wheel assembly and piled my equipment alongside, ready for collection. The word refuse (as in rubbish) comes to mind — it looked as if a fly-tipper had been at work. The useless paddles looked the pick of the pile. With time to kill I brought my log up to date with a moan about my body, which seemed to be falling to bits. *'Feet worn raw by flip-flops. Bites itch. Thigh stiff. Back above shoulder-blades — torn muscles? — like electric current dancing . . .'*

STAINED GLASS MIRROR

Robin arrived at the old bridge bearing wondrous gifts — dry jeans, dry shirt and deliciously dry socks. Before changing, I once more stepped into the river. With Robin assisting from a grassy mid-bank location, overhung with low leafy branches, we raised the water-logged dinghy and placed it, scarred bottom uppermost, on that delightful spot. Had the weather been kinder, I could have spent a blissful night camping there.

With my bags and wheel assembly loaded, the Fiesta headed eastwards, somewhere near Exeter, towards narrow country lanes and a large amp.

A PUB TOO FAR
(Nether Bridge to Greystone Bridge)

Two days after returning from the river I was outside on the terrace washing my muddy sleeping-bag in a white, half dustbin-sized, plastic container. It had been used just once for producing home-brew. The cloudy liquid that covered the soaking bag had characteristics of my first and last brewing experience. Taste may well have been one of them.

I photographed my abused feet. They were exposed to the elements at the time — on account of the water sluicing about as the weighty wet sleeping bag was hoisted on to the clothes-line. The record of the raw patches, where the flip-flop straps had rubbed, would add to the 'Over and Out' file. To the accompaniment of amplified tortured electrical sounds squealing from an upstairs window, I photographed 'Two Sad Feet'. Unlike the 'music', the bruises — Bude temple and Welcombe thigh, were unobtrusive and fading fast.

We will leave this domestic scene — the characters having returned from their riverside rendezvous. One was blissfully content, the other wished a large amplifier was still in the depths of Devonshire.

To minimise future 'Tamar foot' problems I journeyed to Truro to buy some 'super sandals' — the type that had arrangements of adjustable webbing attached to an off-road treaded sole.

Captain's log, Sat 30th July *'Feet healing — continue, or perhaps finish — (dare I think it!!) the voyage, in a few days. Must collect oars etc. Will use red box no crunch crumbs in bottom of damp plastic bag with paraphernalia. Remember 'swiss roll' for I may find myself on stony ground, again. Take some exciting foodstuffs . . .'*

That evening I sat in my gallery with a pint of H S D (Hicks Special Draught, St Austell Brewery) known affectionately as High Speed Diesel. Pouring over Landranger 201 I was a little peeved finding just one pub close to the river on the twenty three mile stretch (about 13 crow miles) still to be traversed. At this point I must state that the venture was in no way fuelled by alcohol — no booze was ever on board during any of the trips; honest.

The Monday was one of misty rain. Tuesday — *'Through the rain and mist to Darracott to collect oars . . .'* I checked Epic on the way. *'. . . looked not too bad from . . . the bridge — lounging casually by the river under the green* (leafy) *canopy.'* Closer inspection showed the hull, round the centre-board slot, had been stripped of paint and the ply deeply gouged after the miles of dragging. Evidence of early yolk-yellow paintwork was revealed where the blue and white had worn away. Wednesday afternoon, August 3rd, heavy rain. Thursday, change 'super sandals' for a cut-price pair from the market. Those costing five times as much had nylon threads, hot-cut, leaving wicked little pointy bits under the straps. I could imagine the damage such defects might do to delicate, soused white feet.

'12:44 P.M. Aug 5th. Robin chauffeur. Quite nervous (me) *this A.M.'* On our way back to Epic we stopped at St Austell to purchase a glass-fibre repair kit and brushes (for use with same). On to Bugle for a pair of scissors that we forgot to buy at St Austell. The bargain price of the Far Eastern product, costing no more than an expensive half pint of beer, was a clue to their worth. They were eleven inches long, had orange plastic covered thumb and finger holes and were sealed behind clear plastic on a printed card — a cunning sales ploy. When unpacked, the scissors showed signs of non-suitability for my purpose and for any other that involved cutting. An unhealthy rattle was a give-away to flimsy engineering. Uri Geller could have found a use for them. The brushes were a good buy though. There were six assorted in the pack, the biggest one being two and a half inches wide.

Robin dropped me off and I set about repairing Epic. Within forty-five minutes I had applied five mixes of resin and glass. The rather too coarse glass fibre sheet was torn apart using the 'Chinese tongs'. *'Sitting by Tamar, Nether Br. — Spiky glass fingers. Hate starting with sticky fingers. Sticking together — looks like rain. Photo from bridge — see the rapids? Fish rose — soon be away from traffic . . .'*

To pass the time of day, while the repair set, I meandered a clockwise circuit of the bridges. I read the plaque on 'my' bridge — 'Higher New Bridge 1504 A.D.' So the newer bypass bridge is the Nether Bridge. I wonder if it will last five hundred years.

'Not raining . . . had sandwich and banana and water — bottle broached! Repair still sticky — wonder if it matters — I'll give it till 1:45! p.m. Think I will have a Mars — brought the red box this time — soon be no food left. 1:55 still tacky . . .'

At 2:10 I turned Epic over and slid her down the steep grassy bank back into the river. The painter was casually looped round a branch and the little dinghy lay against the bank whilst I loaded. Within ten minutes I had unhitched and scrambled down into the cool Tamar, christening my cheap, sturdy looking and hopefully easy-on-my-feet sandals. Though I entered the river towards the end of that long deep-water pool, there was still thirty yards or so of knee-deep water for me to drift on before the first rapids. I stepped into Epic and hoped for more of the same — for the Tamar was soon to be joined by more and more ditches, brooks and rivers. The rivers Carey, Kensey and Lyd were to boost the flow within the next four miles (two and a bit crow). Water swilled over my feet — again I had failed to replace the bung. Perhaps I should have a check-list — boat, bananas, bung, bailer.

Besides the oars and red picnic box my inventory included the large, slightly grubby sail-bag. It would keep together such items as sleeping bag, clothes bag, jumper and 'swiss roll'. On the bolstered bag I would recline as Epic reached more and more 'floating' pools.

STONE PILLAR

' . . . a reminder of a disused railway . . . '

In the following days I hoped to repeat those blissful moments enjoyed after I first stepped into Epic on the River Fowey. '. . . I lay on my back . . . watched the mast turn lazy circles against a few cotton wool clouds'. There would be more paddling and pushing but I still relished the final confrontation with the Tamar.

'Drizzle! mostly walking / dragging rap. (rapids) *every 5 min 3·00 Drifting now for a min. absolute quiet. No — cows munching — thats all.'*

Producing such notes — memory aids for this and the previous Epic books was not a chore. During painting expeditions in the past, to Spain, Portugal, Morocco and Turkey, I had kept diaries for my own satisfaction. From the information in the Turkey diary I produced my first illustrated book. When writing a few paragraphs — background information to be displayed at the exhibition of Bosphorus paintings, the whole story tumbled forth — triggered by the location notes.

I recently unearthed a battered notebook that reveals the 'plot' of a two week holiday involving four young men (late teens) and an old, low-slung black Citroen — with mud-guards and running-boards. From the time we had to lift the car over a slight angle on the ramp — to get the low-slung, overloaded car onto the ferry, to the fan slicing through the radiator incident, outside Lords Cricket Ground on our return, I jotted a few snippets. e.g. Turning in through a gateway.

"Have we missed the wall?"

"Yes (a scraping sound rent the air) most of it."

Back in the swim; I slowly ticked off the remaining miles. Not long after leaving behind a stone pillar — a reminder of a disused railway, I noted, *'3:45 sewage wks outlet looked cleanish'.* I stepped onto the right-hand side of a slightly downward curved concrete weir. The flow passed swiftly over the central section — to aerate the river I supposed. I allowed Epic to ride down the concentrated flow, then pulled the dinghy against the lower side of the weir and stepped back on board. That area of the riverbed was furred with a slimy brown contamination. I had been scathing about the poor old Tamar before — bemoaning its lack of volume when I should have been praising the quality. Paddling in the 'brown' was most off-putting. I was pleased to record that a few hundred yards downstream, the fast flowing river was clear of all traces of Launceston's sanitary arrangement.

At 4:00 I passed beneath a wide, shallow arched road bridge — a crow mile and a bit east of Launceston. There was a *'lot of walking'* and at *'4:15 Rain (Slight)'.* A third of a mile and fifteen minutes later, the lofty concrete slab of the A30 hove in view. The structure was soon out of sight but the audio infringement was significant and prolonged.

'Mars/water. Not quite so gloomy. (I referred to the weather)
5:45. Still hear A.30
6:00   ..   ..   ..   sunny periods   6:10 R.Lyd . . .'

The considerable addition of the extra River Lyd water did not help matters a great deal — the fall of the river being too steep to allow for even small boat navigation. Long stretches of silvery rapids, punctuated with great numbers of large angular rocks — two to three feet across, were the norm. Trees skirted the river down most of its length. Some fields were edged with trees along the river bank allowing extra brightness to add more sparkle to already scintillating scenes. More dense vegetation presented darker, mysterious views.

When deciding on the river journey, in order to enjoy and record the landscape, I had no idea I might be planning to trespass. At the time I was happily, blissfully ignorant. I was to be informed in due course that I was not entirely welcome.

Though not really difficult, and in no way dangerous, the advancement of Epic was still very time consuming. The new 'wide look' Tamar began to show 'hidden depths' — *'6:15*(pm) *rushed down rapid — hang on back to lift myself dry!'* To avoid soakings it was necessary to ride straight-armed, with hands gripping the tipped down transom and legs dangling till foot, shin or knee made contact. Had that technique been used at 7:35 I would not have holed Epic again. With a bit of effort I could have got out of the dinghy as it gathered speed before rushing through a gap at the end of a roughly dammed pool. My weight, as the tender Epic hit a submerged rock, was the problem. After the crunch I sat on the transom, feet inboard, and drifted downstream. Keeping the new piercing above water-level I arrived at the next barrier/dam where another repair, in the pre-described manner, was effected. The second taped patch abutted the first.

By 8:15 Epic was baled out and tidied up, and I was watered and 'Marsed'. There were three man-made dams or weirs to negotiate before I reached Greystone Bridge. The random stone structures, with central breaching, were circumvented by aiming Epic nose first into the break while I, standing on the dam, held a long slack painter to tow the dinghy to quiet water.

With the longed for bridge in sight at the end of a long pool, I came upon a weir that led to fast, tumbling water below. I deemed it prudent to restrain Epic with a line and lower away slowly, stern-first over the confused turbulence while I stood in the river, well back from the slippery, boulder barrier. I was getting used to variations of this procedure. With my dam-buster safely in the side shallows I picked my way precariously through the pushing current to the bank. The river was becoming stroppy.

With great happiness I wrote, *'Greystone 8:40pm'*. All was quiet, as if I had rented the river for my sole use. It was early August yet no one was about. Not a single dreamer peering down from the bridge, wishing vague shapes of swaying weeds into wondrous trout or whopping salmon. On that peaceful, wind-less evening I rowed with leisurely strokes beneath the central arch and turned back upstream to glide onto a small, steep, mud and shingle Devon 'beach', beneath the bridge. To reduce further waterlogging I wedged my roller logs under the stern to raise Epic out of the river.

Next on the agenda was a hearty meal. The OS revealed three options — each a three mile plus hike. Rejecting Launceston in favour of pastures new, I decided on the Devonshire village of Milton Abbot over the Cornish Treburley. I do not remember my reasoning — both were blessed with PH's (pubs). The country pubs were a little risky regarding food availability at that late hour.

There were a few yards of wet undergrowth and muddy terrain to negotiate before reaching the road at the end of the bridge. I carried my trainers and socks and after clambering over the parapet, replaced wet sandals with the dry footwear. I dropped the sandals back down into the field for collection later. With jumper and painting bag over my shoulders I set off at a brisk pace, hoping to reach the PH by 10:00. Despite the exertion in making the steep, winding climb (six hundred feet) I soon found it necessary to put on my jumper, for a dusk chill had set in. Well before reaching the village I was hurrying along in complete darkness. Paleish naked legs flashed my presence to unseen eyes behind blinding headlights. The motorists raced after their patch of light while I played guess the way for a few seconds.

After fifty-four minutes I entered the Edgcumbe Arms. It was exactly 10:00. The comprehensive menu suggested pre-prepared meals but I was not fussy. Customers more enthusiastic for food, of any description, do not exist. I addressed the lady at the food counter. "Hello, may I have . . . "

" . . . last orders at ten." she said, with some definition. It was one minute past ten by then. Perhaps she thought I had been admiring the bill of fare for future reference.

" . . . just a sandwich . . . "

"No . . . chef's just left . . ."

"I've walked especially from Greystone . . . very hungry . . . "

She went to ask the boss. You just have to be polite, pleasant of manner and smile — it seldom fails. She returned.

"No . . ." she said. ". . . he said would you like a Peperami?"

'Sod me!!' I exclaimed later to my log-book.

I declined the spiced stick. Feeling decidedly out of place I joined the merry throng in the bar. The company, two pints of 6X and three packets of crisps did not restore my well-being. I fumed back to Epic. In the corner of a dark damp field, an unhappy troll slipped into cold wet sandals and skulked back under the bridge. Smile and the whole world smiles with you; on occasions. I wonder what the PH at Treburley is like.

GREYSTONE BRIDGE

' . . . an unhappy troll slipped into cold wet sandals and skulked back under the bridge.'

BOLSHIE FISHERMEN
(Greystone Bridge to Horsebridge)

Under the arch, above the one in which Epic was housed, I made camp. The sloping ground was lump free and the cave-like den was too enclosed to allow vegetation to grow. Together with the 'swiss roll', a larger piece of polythene than last time and the absence of driving rain, I was assured a comfortable and restful night. An extremely heavy dew caused spasmodic drops to fall from the vaulted ceiling. Following my recent experience, the odd spots, far from bothering me, emphasized the near perfection of my situation.

I was reluctant to leave the warmth of my grotto. *'Sat.6th Aug. 7:45 Breakfast in Bag. 8.30 Sun breaking through. Walk in river for photos. Not v.cold. Patches on hull seem O.K. 8:45 off to first rapid 30yds away !! 9:00 Br. disappears — stand up and one oar laze my way down a long (300 yds) dark silent greenish pool — quiet — car noise recedes — heaven. 9:07 2nd rapids . . .'*

It was at that 'seven minute pool' or perhaps the one after it that I noticed simple wooden steps. They angled slightly outwards, down the six foot bank into the water. I thought how agreeable the scene was — reflected geometry contrasting with nature's glorious randomness. I did not know at the time, but such features could strike fear into a semi-hardened troll.

My heavenly drifts were due to an increasing number of man-made dam/weirs. Many were honest stone constructions but others suffered blight from an insensitive use of concrete. At 9:45 I gently rowed towards a low, flat-topped stone dam that constricted the river from about fifty feet down to twelve. I was within twenty yards or so of the narrows when I first heard the telltale 'sssh' of what turned into a rumbling, weir warning. My sedate progress was halted for a while. I stepped onto the dam near the Devon bank and walked along the top to inspect the furious white churning below the three foot drop. Epic had to be manhandled over the dam. I unloaded Epic and placed the contents on the dam top. It was a straightforward task to lift the bow onto the ledge, drag the boat up to a balanced position, swing it round and tip it stern-first down to the lower level, then gently lower away with the painter. Who needs locks?

An hour later I approached another breached dam. This one was similar but funnelled water through in a speedy flow — without a waterfall. Not wishing to ride through the gap at speed, or manhandle the boat over the dam and the large area of rough shale below, I decided to walk in the river and guide Epic from behind. All went well till the force of Tamar carried me through the gap before I could get into position to ride on the stern using the straight armed technique. Wet to the waist, I pulled Epic onto the shale beach.

That picturesque spot, well lit — having an empty field behind, was an ideal location to produce a painting. Fast, swirly, light reflecting water slid into a dark void under a green canopy. There, behind a low bank, seated on a rock, with my soaked shorts lying, drying on the sun-warmed ground, I set out my painting equipment.

Not only did the gentle rush of water have a soothing effect, it also drowned the sound of the approaching 'enemy'. Range Rover access, I was about to find out, was never far away in the occupied territory. Watercolours were squeezed onto the palette and river-water filled my water-pot which hung from a twig of driftwood. With poised brush — for there is more calculating than applying pigment, I contemplated strategy.

I did not hear the diesel engine or the voices of the fishermen till they were nearly upon me. Persons, I had not expected. Big Billy Goat Gruff would have been more welcome. Had my shorts been less dry and my reactions slower than Jack Flash, my explaining would have been even more implausible.

". . . private property . . . we are going to fish . . ."

"I did not intend to use your bank . . . got wet, I decided to do a painting. I hope that is O.K.?"

"No, it is private . . . "

"Where am I?"

The merest trace of confusion sounded in the elderly gentleman's voice. I was being spoken at by a very indignant, 'huntin, shootin, fishin', archetype.

". . . Endsleigh fishing . . ."

He found it difficult to converse with one who did not know where he was. With little more 'discussion' I hurriedly packed away my things and set off, post-haste, to enjoy a rare and most welcome minute of rowing. A young man (sixteenish) stood silently by his irate senior as the farce unfolded. But for him, I may have been more vocal. My defence may have been flawed, but had my admonisher cared to listen to my explanation, the interlude could have been less confrontational. When the fisherman relates his version of this particular 'one that got away', I will no doubt be cited as a flagrant trespasser.

Until that moment it had not occurred to me that the river would be out of bounds or that I would be wished elsewhere during the trip. After all, I was not taking liberties with concrete, taking a four-wheel drive through peaceful countryside, or festooning trees with fly-fishing lines.

During the next two hours Epic passed through glorious landscapes. Red stone cliffs, draped with ferns and mosses, were topped by dense wooded slopes. The lie of the land ensured a great deal of dinghy dragging down rapids, interspersed with a little deep water floating.

From time to time I glimpsed large-headed, long necked, sleek black birds about a foot in length (shags). With their harpoon bills they had the appearance of great fishers. They kept a wary distance — obviously unwelcome in the neighbourhood because of their diet. I empathised.

Another dam hove in view. It funnelled fast water into a long, wide pool. In slack water behind the Devon side of the dam a dinghy was held on station by an oarsman while a fisherman cast a fly across the river towards overhanging trees. The line was taken down-river by the current and the angler recast. Not wishing to interrupt proceedings, I parked Epic a little way above the dam against the opposite bank, sat on a log and ate a Mars bar.

During a lull in the activity I made my way to the lip of the breach. The occupants of the dinghy, which was larger than mine, ordered me to cross the river and pass behind them. The fast water claimed Epic — I had no choice but to carry on through the gap. Keeping well in towards the trees on the Cornwall side I silently drifted on. Though my behaviour was reverential I still received abuse for my unintentional manoeuvre. Thankfully, the reserve troops were on the opposite bank. It was a pity that so many of the 'sportsmen' were antagonistic. Some of the enjoyment of that end of the voyage experience was taken away.

The next but one dam/weir took a full fifteen minutes to negotiate, though I worked at pace, fearing fishermen intervention. Stone steps led down to ten foot wide sloping, rocky beaches that flanked the dam. My ears were tuned to pick up the first sound of danger — for by that time I feared there might be a price on my head. From the oars, rocks and my log collection I hastily fashioned a crude ramp and heaved the unladen dinghy over the dam and back into the river. Luckily there was no clink of cold cutlass steel against stone steps.

At 2:20 I hitched Epic to an overhanging branch midway along a deep pool. Within the two-hundred yards of restricted vision, the trees crowding the waterway receded from dark greens to an atmospheric blue-blackness. Cutting the mid distance, a narrow slash of bright, rushing silvery water added a strong feature to the composition. I spent a little under an hour painting a watery 'Tamar-colour'. Epic had let in a few pints and it was convenient painting from a 'water pot'. While my creation dried in the warm air I lunched on diluted orange juice and a Crunchy bar.

The painting had put me in better heart. Better still, the tension eased when I drifted past two fishermen. We exchanged friendly "Good afternoons" and I rowed by feeling more at one with the world. Perhaps I had been unlucky earlier — meeting up with bolshie factions.

Many more dams were circumvented. When two or three of a similar construction were in close proximity, the random beauty of the river was totally destroyed. As the general public cannot view that section of the Tamar, perhaps it does not matter.

There were a lot of wide, fast flowing stretches where I had to resist the temptation to ride with Epic. The heavy flood-resisting rocks that were visible were not the problem — the danger came from those just below the surface, of which there were great numbers.

With trepidation only partly allayed I waded down rapids towards another group of fishermen. Excited animation broke out and I felt assured of a trouble free passage. A bent rod juddered, stabbing in the direction of a hooked fish. Feeling relaxed, I waited till the netting and victorious clambering up the bank had ensured no escape for the salmon. Vacating the scene as discreetly as is possible when towing a ten foot white dinghy, I expected to be ignored by the successful angler.

"And where are you going?"

"Morwellham Quay." I shouted, having nothing to hide.

The salmon catcher cupped a hand to his ear. The rushing water and his congratulatory entourage may have drowned my reply.

PAINTING FROM EPIC

'I spent a little under an hour painting a watery 'Tamar-colour'. Epic had let in a few pints and it was convenient painting from a 'water pot'.'

"Morwellham Quay." I roared.

There was no easy reply to my positive answer that an elated fisherman could make without ruining his moment of triumph. My interrogator turned away and bashed the salmon to death with a metal rod. I got off lightly, but still communed with my log in aggressive terms. *'He gave no reply! Bastard. With a fish I thought he must be friendly! (4:30ish)'*

The Endsleigh zone, I believed was behind me when I asked a civilian, standing in neutral territory on the Cornwall bank, where the Horsebridge was. The crossing which had a PH nearby was less than a mile away, with only one weir en route. At 7:30 I arrived at the Horsebridge, which was almost identical to Greystone Bridge, and made myself at home. Epic was soon perched on one of the broad stone foundations that was partly exposed due to the low river level. The sloping stone ledge was within easy leaping distance of the shore. I hopped over to the rocky foreshore and clambered up the steep grassy bank — to the downstream, Devon end of the bridge. Not wishing to advertise the fact that I was a river traveller, I decided to nip on to the roadway quickly and act in a casual manner. In a trice I was up and on the parapet with legs dangling nonchalantly road-side. I casually leant back. It was unfortunate that the stone capping was deceptively narrow. You would expect a little wear since 1437. My palms met thin air, my legs flew over my head and I crashed back down onto the slope. My landing on feet then knees was extremely lucky — only losing marks for a pronounced stumble.

The Royal Inn (combining Horsebridge Brewery) was just a step away upstream. I had arrived at a respectable hour for leisurely dining. Things were looking up and I started at the pinnacle — with a pint of the pub's own brew. The following day I hoped to conclude the circumnavigation so I decided to celebrate in style. A couple at the bar ordered venison in red wine. There was only one portion left. I could have eaten a horse but settled for the venison. The remains of the deer were few and the red wine sauce had a burnt, warmed up and watered down once too often taste. I had not expected a miracle, but turning wine into water was too much. Together with the accompanying salad, ample lettuce topped with a small sculpted vegetable, the fare rated poorly in both quality and quantity to the three bags of crisps taken the previous night. The lettuce leaves I added to the sauce. Salted and peppered it was still more visual than fortifying. Perhaps I should have made a fuss, but it had been a bad day for discourse and I had no wish to create waves.*

An early night was not a bad idea. Rapidly descending 'mount celebration' I cut short my Saturday night out and trolled back to my riverside lair. Later, faint conversations drifted my way as the 'chucking out' was celebrated. Car engines sounded for a while, then I was left in silence, beside the still Tamar.

---

* *Later I returned to the Royal Inn and found it under new management. Not mentioning the reason for my research I passed a pleasant evening and dined royally.*

86

DAM
(Horsebridge to Morwellham Quay)

Sunday morning — up at 5:30, off at 6:00. A thick silent mist confused reality. The river may not have existed — I could have spent the night beside a pond. Epic soon drifted into the real world and the first rapids. The river sounded its chuckling challenge and the bridge was enveloped in grey. The dinghy nudged a heavy stone and I tentatively dipped a dry sandalled foot into a slightly chilled Tamar.

Loneliness was never a problem. I usually work alone. It would be a dull painter who would not be content in the 'company' of such glorious landscape. (I will be 'fluttering and dancing in the breeze' next.) When on the move there was little time for day-dreaming. On a few occasions I had to retrace my course. Heaving back over hard won ground, back-tracking past rocks marked with 'Epic white', was a strict reminder to concentrate.

From 6:40 an anxious twenty minutes ensued. I sighted a fishermen's encampment off the starboard bow. Tents and a Range Rover were in full view, in a field, fifteen yards or so from the Devon bank and about forty yards away from the dam wall over which Epic's front half protruded. I hoped the party were sleeping soundly. The water that thundered through the gap in the centre of the dam drowned out the bangings and rumblings caused by the unladen boat being dragged across the flattish shelves of rock on oars and logs. With great exertion I rushed Epic to the edge of the surging flow. After loading I escaped under oar-power, having passed close in to the bank, out of sight of the fishermen. I could relax for a while. *'I DREAD FISHERMEN'*, I recorded.

A few hundred yards downstream on another long pool I photographed the tranquil splendour of a scene reflected in the still water. The fully leafed trees that overhung both banks paled into the misty distance. Low down, above the barely discernible, furthermost winding of the river, a round object hove into view. I quickly took a second picture. What luck to witness such a scene; and to have my camera poised at that precise moment. There were no more than a couple of seconds before the sphere passed out of sight, behind the trees, but I snapped the second time as the hot air balloon was in the centre of the small 'target' area. It would be a prize-winning sensation. It was not — only the number on the negative tells which was the second shot. My camera lies.

Two hours passed. I passed weirs and shallows, but no fishermen. Perhaps Sundays are truce days — lucky for me and the salmon. Fortune favoured me at the next dam. A low, planked foot-bridge linking the Devon bank to the dam had just enough room for Epic to be squeezed beneath. The following short stretch of shallow rapids had sufficient flow for me to ease the dinghy, with little fuss, back to the main river.

'. . . this is the most difficult yet 9:30 4th weir must unload and drop Epic over wall!!' As I tried to lower the bow down into the shallow water from the four foot lip, my right foot slipped into an unnoticed crevice. Trapped up to my knee for a short while I was fortunate not to damage leg-parts during the operation.

'10:45 Just over another dam then weir then rapids . . . Now big rocks — fast water.!! 1 pint or so leak every 5-10 minutes or so!' There was a greater flow outside the boat and it seemed to be over steeper ground. Often there were wide stretches where it was difficult to stand. The powerful weight of water made it tricky to thread my way between slippery rocks while restraining Epic. Despite severe treatment my 'cheapo' sandals stood the test very well — they were as good as new to the end, and extremely clean. The boat would occasionally decide on a route for itself. This occurred when the side of the dinghy pivoted against a rock and I could not tip the balance in my favour. Epic would head off to boulder traps which necessitated extrication using the 'oar-ramp' method.

'. . . slipped over again . . . 11:30 end of 1st 'Big Rock Rapids?'' Then 200 yds downstream, more of the same. '12:20 Through next 'Boulder Run' (600 yds long) . . .' One and a half minutes later I faced a further half-hour negotiating large rocks. Those water-smoothed examples, like giant grey dumplings, rose up to five feet out of the river. When the rounded rocks were too plentiful and blocked the way, my deceptively strong, trusty oars were brought into play again. '1" water in bottom. 1:04 Row — last of the boulders? . . . shorts wet — long pool I hope. Nearly there!' My notes suggest I was pretty tired at the time. I expect I was exhausted but did not feel it — on auto pilot again.

Rowing. No problems — just rowing. I had waited a long time. '1:25 Under the Bridge can't believe it. I thought it was hours away.' (I left the space to add the name later. It is another New Bridge — as imaginative as Gull Rock.) The OS indicated a mile to go before the final weir. That last bridge — the first above the tidal Tamar was a dead ringer of the previous two — as if the same contractors, fifteenth century McAlpines had constructed all three in a discount package.

'River became v. still. Lots of leaves turning yellow floating — stalks up — like little boats. Wind is blowing me back upstream . . .' (I had stopped to make notes.) On the last page of my log book I had drawn a couple of leaf boats and a floating lager can that happened to be there. The few shorthand marks recorded the information rapidly — perhaps not painting a thousand words but the slightest glance takes me back to the river. My runes were symbolic — the autumn of the voyage and time to celebrate with a swift pint. No, I must not be flippant, it was quite an emotional time.

Those few hundred yards, when I thought all surprises were behind me, were rowed at a leisurely pace. In peaceful privacy and contemplative mood I savoured those moments. The conclusion of my journey was nigh. '1:42 do I hear the weir — or wind in trees?' (I was being serious.) A little later, 'It is the weir — bloody Hell'.

EPIC IN FAST WATER

'There was a greater flow outside the boat and it seemed to be over steeper ground.'

The tree-cover on the Devon side gave way to a red-stone bluff, topped with a few conifers — it had a Rhineland feel. A structure on the Cornwall side turned out not to be a schloss but a concrete and steel affair for counting fish. The device, which would hurry the unsuspecting salmon towards a possible encounter with a metal bar, was set beside a construction much larger than a regular weir.

A few seconds later I realized I was floating towards the edge of a really big dam. When a few yards from the lip I looked over towards a group of particular trees. They were about a quarter of a mile away and shielded the cottage I had passed by on my way up from Morwellham on the first trip. From there, before turning seawards, I had taken a photograph showing a distant weir which I thought was Gunnislake Dam. I had seen the dam three years before, when contemplating launching Epic in the pool below it, but paid little attention, never thinking that one day I would be taking a boat over it. The strip of white water in the picture suggested I would not have a problem descending to the upper tidal reach.

The tremendous roar as the river crashed over the dam prepared me for an alarming sight. I had not expected anything of that magnitude. At first there seemed no way to get Epic and myself safely down the fall. Victoria, Niagara and splintered barrels came to mind. The unusual low level of the river had increased the drop to the pool below to eight feet, though it seemed much more.

Towards the Devon side of the dam a substantial fish-ladder had been constructed to enable athletic salmon to return to their spawning grounds — that was before the sissy by-pass counter had been installed. Two parallel walls, one foot wide and four feet apart, ran out twenty five feet or so, beyond the roughest water at the base of the dam. The wall-tops, with a one in five downward slope, ended just four feet above the swift flowing water. Four churning pools were sectioned off between the walls. They were fed in some cunning way — for although little water seemed to enter, each chamber boiled as though giant mixers were set at whipping speed. Thick wet spongy weed grew on the precarious slopes.

Epic remained afloat at the lip of the dam, restrained by the end of the concrete fish-ladder that stood a couple of inches proud of the water. I stepped gingerly onto the small area of weedy concrete, and with due care, balanced my gear there. With a 'what the hell' cavalier approach, I dragged Epic up onto the Devon-side 'slide' and boldly went. Half expecting my abused boat to take a nose dive, I edged Epic onto the incline.

Even if Epic had been mortally wounded I would still have reached my goal — just a few hundred yards away. Fortunately, my treaded sandals and the dinghy's scarred bottom had purchase enough for a controlled descent. At the end of the sloping wall I pivoted Epic and re-launched stern first. With Epic tethered from a convenient fixing on the side of the wall I made a couple of trips up the slope to collect the gear. I tossed the sail-bag into the dinghy and after lowering myself in, reached up for the red box and oars.

I noted the time, *'2:20'*, then rowed two hundred yards past the Cornwall side of a wooded island down to the final weir. The upstream pointing, shallow 'V' shaped construction, that I had thought was Gunnislake Dam, I negotiated with practised ease.

The transition to tidal waters was undertaken at warp speed. The feeling that I should not be using the river authority's fixtures for recreational purposes spurred me on. My desire was to exit the dam area without delay — for I felt like a fugitive. Had I been able to relax it would have been sensible to wait for the flood tide and enjoy two miles of carefree rowing down to Morwellham.

A stiff breeze was blowing upriver. After a few oar-strokes I decided it was easier to walk. With Epic in tow I passed the point reached four years earlier and, well, just carried on walking. Soon I arrived at the spot from where, as near as I could remember, I had taken a picture of Lock Cottage on the first trip. Then 'the river on which Epic slowly revolved was brimful and coffee coloured after the rains'. This time, the dinghy showing a grubby tide-mark was grounded in the shallows. I could stand back and photograph the location again. The second picture includes, what is probably, the only sailing boat to have been taken right round the County border.

Before bringing my little dinghy to the Tamar I had hastily applied white paint to the top-sides leaving rough sky-blue capitals, E P I C, on the stern. Though named in jest — a silly way of ensuring an epic voyage, it now seems rather fitting.

Epic, over and out.

Postamble

The circumnavigation was complete. I headed on down towards Morwellham Quay — two 'crow' miles away. Within seconds the swishing sound of fine gravel on the hull foretold grounding. I nipped over the side and continued on foot for a while, till the river got deeper; I always knew it would.

My last logbook entry, *'Morwellham 3:30 — Mars — lay in sun rest on kit-bag — NO I arrived as the tide came in — could not stay wedged into mud — floated off Tied up 4:15 — 4:30ish — bit sad really!. . .'*

In its own time the Tamar rose, allowing me to row onto the flooded slip where the hulk of an old Tamar barge had rested. It was alongside the salvaged vessel, which was at an early stage of renovation, that I introduced Epic to the river. At the side of the slip I added my log collection to off-cuts of shipbuilding timber. The 'Lynher' had been moved some twenty yards away from the slip. There, Charlie who had reclaimed the old boat from the mud, and Ralph, were at the planking stage. Though time consuming, it is a rewarding labour of love — sort of like circumnavigating.

David Weston, Mevagissey.

January 1998.

'Down in the studio, where I often produce watercolours of the cluttered shelves, I sorted out materials to create my transporter.'